The Infra-Red Cook Book

Kathy Barnes has been demonstratin[...]
the catering and domestic trade for [...]
widely known as the leading expert [...]

Other cookery books available in Pan

KATHY
BARNES

The
Infra-Red
Cook Book

Pan Books London and Sydney

First published 1980 by Canongate Publishers Ltd
and simultaneously in paperback by Pan Books Ltd,
Cavaye Place, London SW10 9PG
2nd printing 1981
© Kathy Barnes 1980
ISBN 0 330 25966 0
Richard Clay (The Chaucer Press) Ltd, Bungay, Suffolk

to my dear husband, Arnott

Contents

Acknowledgements

The author would like to thank:

Carnethy Butchers, Penicuik
James Gray and Sons, Ironmongers, Edinburgh
John Kelly and Sons, Catering Suppliers, Bonnyrigg
Hartington Engineering Co Ltd, London
Rima Electric Ltd, London

– all of whom either supplied food, allowed the use of
equipment and utensils or the use of their kitchens, thus
enabling me to do the research and testing. I would also like
to thank Bill Mayberry for his help in finding a home for this
book.

Introduction:
the infra-red grill

Advantages

The most immediately obvious advantage infra-red grills have over conventional domestic cookers is their ability to cook the same meals in a fraction of the time. This is likely to be an increasingly important asset, not only because people have less and less time to spend in the kitchen but also because the saving in time also results in a considerable saving in fuel consumption, thus cutting costs. The initial cost of the grill is soon outweighed by such savings. Compare these figures:

items cooked	normal cooker uses	infra-red grill
gammon steak	.330 kWh	.154 kWh
frozen lasagne	1.178	.381
pork chop	.517	.147

It is good to be able to grill a steak in three minutes or bake a swiss roll in five, but an extra bonus in this age of the deep-freeze is no longer having to wait all those hours for food to thaw; you just put it straight into your infra-red grill, and the food retains the best possible flavour in the cooking.

It must be emphasized that the time saved by using infra-red grills is not by any means to the detriment of the food; the flavour and texture will be just as good, indeed often better,

11

than if cooked the more conventional way. All natural flavours are retained as the food is cooked all the way through without losing any of its juices in the process.

There are various different makes of grill but they are all highly versatile, being lightweight and portable. They can be placed at any height and in small spaces and are thus particularly excellent for the elderly, disabled and those living in bedsitters.

How it works

With a conventional cooker, if you try to cook anything fast the outside of the food tends to burn before the inside is properly cooked. With the infra-red grill, the outside of say, a piece of steak is rapidly cooked by the generous heat supplied by the hot plates above and below the meat; meanwhile the inside of the meat is cooking just as fast because of the additional infra-red rays. These rays are of a frequency which makes them invisible to the human eye but which also means that the heat is much more concentrated than with ordinary heat radiation – so the food cooks all the way through in a very short time: the penetration power of the infra-red rays is in no way hindered by the outer skin of the steak. All the natural flavours are retained as the food cooks in its own juices, and an excellent texture is achieved. Infra-red cooking is completely safe and will in no way endanger health.

How to use the grill

All the infra-red grills vary slightly in performance so it is absolutely essential and important that you read thoroughly the instructions and recipe booklets supplied with your cooker.

Put your grill on a level surface and avoid trailing the flex or allowing it to touch the cooker. You need a three-point plug (BS 1363) and not less than a 13 amp rating.

Before using the grill for the first time, wipe it with warm soapy water and a soft sponge or cloth. Wipe the teflon plates very, very lightly with cooking oil.

Voltage drops can affect cooking times. This is often reflected in the room lights or TV brightness. If the voltage is low adjust the cooking temperature to a higher setting (if you are using a temperature-controlled grill).

Allow 7–10 minutes with the plates closed for your grill to heat up. When the correct temperature is obtained the indicator light will go out.

When cooking directly between the non-stick plates the food should be placed on the lower plate and the upper plate lowered on to the food.

A baking tray should be provided with your infra-red grill. When cooking soft foods, such as fish, eggs and vegetables, use the baking tray and place it on the bottom hot plate before lowering the top hot plate until it rests on the rim of the baking tray. You can also use your own small cooking dishes or trays; round, oval or square ones will work providing they fit your cooker. However, these must obviously be heat-proof so china, earthenware or glass will not do.

Baking foil can safely be used over food cooking in grills to avoid spitting and splashing. This is mentioned in several of the recipes throughout the book but unless specific timing is given the use of foil will lengthen cooking times.

The recipes in this book state the times for cooking on grills with removable plates. For grills with *non-removable* plates reduce the times stated in the recipes by *one-third*.

The cooking times given in the recipes are only a rough guide. You will need to get to know your particular grill to gauge

the best results, and it also depends on personal taste
of course.

Remember when following a recipe use either the metric or
the imperial measures throughout. Never try to mix the two.

Each recipe in this book, unless otherwise stated, gives
quantities of ingredients which when combined as the recipe
instructs, will cook the amount of food to fill the standard
infra-red baking tray. The baking tray may for instance only
be large enough for a reasonable steak each for two people
whilst on the other hand allowing for a shepherd's pie for three
or even four people. The recipes therefore vary accordingly.

Cleaning the grill

If your grill has *non-removable* plates:

1 Un-plug the grill
2 While the grill is still warm to the touch, pour off the
   excess fats through the corners of the closed grill and wipe
   it gently with kitchen roll paper
3 Use a nylon dishwashing brush and brush the plates very
   gently with very hot water
4 Squeeze a little washing-up liquid on to the plates and scrub
   gently with the nylon brush
5 Remove all traces of soap from the grill plates by wiping
   them with a damp, soft cloth
6 Plug in and switch on the grill for one minute to
   completely dry off the plates

If your grill has *removable* plates:

Remove the plates when they are cool enough to touch and
soak them in hot water with some detergent. If necessary
scrub them gently with a nylon washing-up brush, rinse
thoroughly under warm water and dry with a soft cloth.

Griddle plates should be wiped with a soft cloth dipped in warm detergent water.

Certain foods such as tomatoes, sauces, spices and various sea foods tend to stain aluminium baking tins. This can be minimized by cleaning them immediately after use. Such staining, however, in no way impairs the efficiency of your cooking tray or the quality of the food prepared. Scouring pads or abrasives may be used to clean the baking tray though *never* to clean the actual grill or you will spoil the non-stick surfaces.

A final word of warning: *never* immerse the grill or the flexible cable in water for cleaning.

Frozen food

Frozen food can be cooked on the infra-red grill in the following way:

Preheat automatic grills

Preheat temperature-controlled grills on the highest setting

Frozen beef steaks

Method 1 Brush the steaks with oil. Season them with salt and pepper. Place them on some buttered foil. Add a few onion rings. Wrap up steaks and onions in foil as a parcel. With the top plate lowered cook for 20–25 minutes.

Method 2 Brush the baking tin with oil and brush the top of the steaks with oil. Add some onion rings. Lower the top of the grill and cook for 20–25 minutes.

Cook frozen lamb chops using method 2, but omitting the onion rings.

Frozen sausage rolls, etc.

Place the rolls in the baking tray and cook with the top plate lowered for 20–25 minutes until browned.

Frozen vegetables

Any kind of frozen vegetable can be cooked in the baking tray with a little water and salt. Cover with baking foil, and with the top plate lowered, cook for 7 minutes or until tender.

Tried and tested models

The recipes throughout the book have been tested on the following models:

Hartington standard automatic – non-removable plate
Hartington chrome, 3-in-1 cooker – automatic with removable plates exposing griddle
Rima temperature-controlled 901 – non-removable plates
Rima temperature-controlled 903 – removable plates
Sunbeam temperature-controlled 1QG/2 – non-removable plates
Sunbeam temperature-controlled 903 – non-removable plates
Philips temperature-controlled – non-removable plates

The only infra-red griddle available at the time the book went to press is the *Hartington* 3-in-1 cooker.

Fish

Kedgeree

Preheat automatic grills
Preheat temperature-controlled grills on highest number

175 g (6 oz) cooked
  smoked haddock
175 g (6 oz) cooked
  long-grained rice
75 g (3 oz) butter
1 small onion, finely
  chopped

2 hardboiled eggs,
  chopped
salt and pepper
1 tablespoon cream or
  evaporated milk
parsley

Melt the butter in a baking tray on the grill. Place the fish in it, lower the top plate of the grill and cook the fish for 5 minutes, then flake it with a fork. Put one of the egg yolks through a sieve and save it to garnish. Add the rest of the hardboiled eggs, rice, cream and salt and pepper. Mix all together. With the top plate lowered cook the kedgeree for 3 minutes. Serve on a hot dish with parsley and the sieved egg yolk.

Cod in cheese sauce

Preheat automatic grills
Preheat temperature-controlled grills on highest number

450 g (1 lb) cod	280 ml ($\frac{1}{2}$ pint) milk
25 g (1 oz) plain flour	50 g (2 oz) grated cheese
50 g (2 oz) butter	a little mustard

Prepare the cheese sauce by melting half the butter in a
saucepan. Remove from the heat and add the milk. Bring to
the boil and stir until it is smooth and thick. Add the cheese
and a little mustard. Meanwhile melt the rest of the butter
in the baking tray, add the cod and, with the top plate
lowered, cook for 5–6 minutes. Add the cheese sauce. Again
lower the top plate and cook for 2 minutes.

Seafood kebabs

Preheat automatic grills
Preheat temperature-controlled grills on highest number

450 g (1 lb) cod or haddock	few black olives, stoned
2 tomatoes	1 tablespoon lemon juice
1 small green pepper	50 g (2 oz) butter, melted
4 kebab skewers	salt and pepper

Cut the fish into chunky pieces. Quarter the tomatoes,
de-seed the pepper and cut the flesh into fairly large pieces.
Place alternate pieces of fish, tomato quarters, pieces of
pepper and whole black olives on to the 4 skewers. Season
well with salt and pepper. Mix the lemon juice and butter
and brush this liberally over the kebabs. Lightly grease a
baking tray and put the kebabs in it. With the top plate

lowered cook for 5–7 minutes. Serve on a bed of boiled and drained rice. Accompany the dish with a green salad.

Grilled fish cakes

Preheat automatic grills
Preheat temperature-controlled grills on highest number

225 g (8 oz) tin tuna or any other fish
salt and pepper
1 tablespoon chopped parsley
340 g (12 oz) potato, cooked and mashed

25 g (1 oz) soft margarine
1 large egg, beaten
1–2 tablespoons cooking oil
breadcrumbs

Drain the fish and mash it up with the chopped parsley, salt and pepper. Mix the margarine with the mashed potato and the fish. Divide the mixture into 8 pieces. Form 8 round cakes. Dip them into the beaten egg then toss them into the breadcrumbs, pressing the crumbs well into the fish cakes. Put the oil in the baking tray. Put in the fish cakes, put the tray on the hot grill, lower the top plate and cook for 3 minutes. Open the grill and turn the cakes over. Again lower the top plate and cook for a further 5 minutes until the cakes brown.

Grilled tuna and spaghetti bake

Preheat automatic grills
Preheat temperature-controlled grills on highest number

340 g (12 oz) tin tuna
fish flaked
2 medium onions, sliced
100 g (4 oz) mushrooms,
sliced
225 g (8 oz) cooked
spaghetti or tinned in
tomato sauce

25 g (1 oz) soft margarine
salt and pepper
pinch of sugar
450 g (1 lb) tin tomatoes
175 g (6 oz) grated
cheddar cheese

Place a baking tray on the grill. Add the margarine and
onions. With the top plate lowered cook for 4 minutes. Open
the grill, add the spaghetti, tuna fish, salt and pepper,
tomatoes and sugar. Cover with the mushrooms and cheese.
Lower the top plate and cook for 8–10 minutes. If the
cheese should stick to the top plate, brush it off immediately
with a nylon dish washing brush.

Tuna fish with rice

Preheat automatic grills
Preheat temperature-controlled grills Rima 901 No 4
Rima 903 No 3
Philips No 4
Sunbeam No 4

200 g (7 oz) tuna fish
225 g (8 oz) long-grain
rice, boiled
1 large onion, chopped

1 small packet of a
frozen vegetable
salt and pepper

Drain the tuna fish and pour the oil into a baking tray. Add
the onion, place the tray on the grill and, with the top plate
lowered, cook the onion for 4 minutes. Chop the tuna fish and
mix with the vegetables (no need to defrost them). Open the
grill and add the rice, tuna and mixed vegetables. Again
lower the top plate and cook for 7 minutes.

Salmon steaks

Preheat automatic grills
Preheat temperature-controlled grills on highest number

2 cm (¾ in) thick salmon steaks
oil
cucumber or hollandaise sauce

Brush both sides of the salmon steaks with oil. Place them
directly on the grill plates. Lower the top of the grill and
cook for 4 minutes. Serve with cucumber or hollandaise
sauce.

Grilled salmon steaks with hollandaise sauce

Preheat automatic grills
Preheat temperature-controlled grills at highest number

4 salmon steaks
75 g (3 oz) butter
salt and pepper
lemon juice

hollandaise sauce

2 tablespoons vinegar
4 tablespoons water
3 egg yolks
175 g (6 oz) soft butter

salt and pepper
lemon juice
few peppercorns

Brush the steaks on both sides with soft butter. Sprinkle them
with salt, pepper and lemon juice. Place the steaks on a
baking tray and, with the top plate lowered, cook them for
3 minutes on each side. Make the sauce by boiling the vinegar,
peppercorns and water in a saucepan for 5 minutes. Strain
through a sieve and add the sieved egg yolks. Whisk over a
low heat until the sauce begins to thicken. Drop small pieces
of butter gradually into the sauce. Season and add a few

21

drops of lemon juice. Garnish the fish with parsley and lemon juice and serve the hollandaise sauce separately.

Normandy trout

Preheat automatic grills
Preheat temperature-controlled grills on highest number

2 trout
50 g (2 oz) butter
1 tablespoon water
squeeze lemon juice
salt and pepper

2 tablespoons chopped
  parsley
2 tablespoons single cream
25 g (1 oz) fresh white
  breadcrumbs

Melt the butter in the baking tray on the lower plate of the grill. Put the trout in the tray. Sprinkle with the water, lemon juice, seasoning and parsley. Cover with cooking foil and, with the top plate lowered, cook for 10 minutes. Open the grill, remove the foil and pour the cream on. Cover with foil again and, with the top plate lowered, cook for 4–5 minutes. Open again and cover with the breadcrumbs. Dot with a little butter, lower the top of the grill and cook without foil for a further 3 minutes. Serve with lemon pieces.

Trout meunière

Preheat automatic grills
Preheat temperature-controlled grills on highest number

1 trout
50 g (2 oz) butter
lemon juice
salt and pepper

Place the butter and trout in a baking tray. Add lemon juice and seasoning. Lower the top of the grill and cook for 5–6 minutes. If frozen trout is used cook for 10–12 minutes.

Kippers in foil

Preheat automatic grills
Preheat temperature-controlled grills on highest number

2 kippers
a little cooking oil
foil

Use a piece of foil double the size of the grill plate. Place 2 kippers with the flesh sides together (as a pair). Oil the foil. Wrap the kippers in a flat parcel, sealing the top and sides. Cook them for 5 minutes with the top plate lowered. Cooked in this way there is no lingering smell of kippers in the kitchen.
Dispose of the foil immediately.

Kipper scramble

Preheat automatic grills
Preheat temperature-controlled grills on highest number

225 g (8 oz) tin John West
  kippers, flaked or fresh
  cooked and boned
  kippers, flaked

25 g (1 oz) soft margarine
4 eggs
2 tablespoons milk
4 slices toast or bread
  salt and pepper

Melt the margarine in a saucepan. Beat the eggs, milk and seasoning thoroughly together. Mix the flaked kippers with the eggs and add them to the margarine. Place the mixture in a baking tray and put it on the grill. With the top plate lowered cook for 15–20 minutes or until set. Pile on to hot buttered toast or bread and serve immediately.

Cider-baked haddock

Preheat automatic grills
Preheat temperature-controlled grills on highest number

450 g (1 lb) fresh haddock
salt and pepper
squeeze of lemon juice
pinch of mixed dried herbs
25 g (1 oz) butter

1 small onion, peeled and
 finely chopped
50 g (2 oz) small mushrooms
150 ml ($\frac{1}{4}$ pint) dry cider
parsley and anchovy fillet
 to garnish, if desired

Remove the skins from the haddock and cut the fillets into 4 portions. Lightly butter the baking tray and put in the fish. Sprinkle it with seasoning, lemon juice and herbs. Add the onions and mushrooms, and pour in the cider. Cover with baking foil and, with the top plate lowered, cook for 15–20 minutes or until fish flakes easily when tested. Serve hot, garnished with anchovies and parsley.

Mackerel pie

Preheat automatic grills
Preheat temperature-controlled grills on highest number

200 g (7 oz) mackerel
 (tinned will do)
tomato sauce if fresh
 fish used
4 slices of toasted bread

1 large onion,
 finely chopped
25 g (1 oz) soft margarine
1 small packet parsley
 sauce mix

Place the baking tray on the grill. Add the margarine and onion. Lower the top of the grill and cook for 4 minutes. Open the grill and add the flaked fish and parsley mix. Again lower the top of the grill and cook for 5 minutes. Cut the hot toast into triangular pieces and decorate the top of the baked fish before serving.

Chicken

Paprika chicken

Preheat automatic grills
Preheat temperature-controlled grills on highest number

1 tablespoon plain flour	1 tablespoon oil
1 teaspoon paprika	225 g (8 oz) tinned
$\frac{1}{4}$ teaspoon salt	sweetcorn
2 chicken legs –	225 g (8 oz) tinned
not too thick	tomatoes
1 tablespoon butter	1 tablespoon chopped parsley

Mix the flour, paprika and salt. Flour the chicken joints with this mixture. Heat the butter and oil in the baking tray. Add the chicken legs and brown them all over in the closed cooker. Add the sweetcorn, tomatoes and parsley. Cover with buttered foil. Lower the top of the grill and cook for 20–25 minutes until tender.

Grilled and devilled left-over chicken

Preheat automatic grills
Preheat temperature-controlled grills on highest number

340 g (12 oz) left-over *cooked* chicken

to devil paste

75 g (3 oz) soft margarine	2 tablespoons sweet chutney
1 teaspoon curry powder	1 teaspoon Worcester sauce
salt and pepper	1 tablespoon tomato purée

Take the chicken off the bone and place it in a baking tray. Beat the soft margarine with the curry powder, seasoning, chutney, sauce and purée. Spread this paste over the chicken. Put the tray on the grill and, with the top plate lowered, cook for 8–10 minutes. Serve with fresh green salad.

Chicken bake

Preheat automatic grills
Preheat temperature-controlled grills on highest number

225 g (8 oz) cooked chicken	4 tomatoes, peeled and
1 tablespoon butter	halved
1 small onion, peeled	salt and pepper
and chopped	1 teaspoon cornflour
½ green pepper, seeded	noodles, cooked
and chopped	2 tablespoons cheddar
	cheese, grated

Melt the butter in a baking tray. Add the onion and green pepper. Lower the top of the grill and cook for 4 minutes. Add the diced chicken, tomatoes, and season well with salt and pepper. Lower the top of the grill and cook for 6–7 minutes. Mix the cornflour to a smooth paste with a little water, stir this into the chicken mixture. Do not close the cooker, but leave the tray on the lower grill for 2 minutes. Serve on a bed of cooked noodles and sprinkle with the grated cheese.

Chicken in lemon sauce

Preheat automatic grills
Preheat temperature-controlled grills on highest number

4 chicken joints, cooked
2 tablespoons butter
1 tablespoon plain flour
150 ml (¼ pint) chicken
  stock
150 ml (¼ pint) milk

¼ teaspoon dried herbs
rind of one lemon, finely
  grated
1 tablespoon lemon juice
salt and pepper
parsley

Remove the chicken flesh from the bones and cut the meat into strips. Melt the butter in the baking tray and add the flour. Lower the top of the cooker and cook for 3–5 minutes. Gradually add the stock and the milk, stirring until very hot. Add the herbs, lemon rind, lemon juice and season with salt and pepper. Add the chicken. With the top plate lowered, cook for 7–10 minutes. Garnish with parsley and serve.

Mock chicken cutlets

Preheat automatic grills
Preheat temperature-controlled grills on highest number

25 g (1 oz) butter or
  margarine
25 g (1 oz) flour
150 ml (¼ pint) milk
4 eggs, hardboiled
  and chopped
100 g (4 oz) ham, cooked
  and diced

salt and pepper
dash of Worcester sauce
dash of soya sauce
egg and breadcrumbs
  for coating
4 pieces macaroni
chopped parsley and
  thyme

Make a sauce by melting most of the butter in a pan and
adding flour. Mix to a smooth paste. Add the milk and bring
to the boil. Add the rest of the ingredients (except for the
egg, breadcrumb coating, and macaroni). Mix well, shape the
mixture into 4 cutlets, coat with some beaten egg and dip in
breadcrumbs. Place a piece of macaroni into the end to
represent the bone.

Melt the small remaining piece of butter or margarine in a
baking tray on the bottom plate of grill. Put the cutlets in
and, with the top plate lowered, cook for 4 minutes. Open
the grill and turn over the cutlets. Again lower the top of the
cooker and cook for a further 4 minutes. Serve on a hot dish,
garnished with chopped parsley.

Quick chicken flan with asparagus

Preheat automatic grills
Preheat temperature-controlled grills on highest number

225 g (8 oz) shortcrust
  pastry
225 g (8 oz) cooked
  chicken pieces
175 ml ($\frac{1}{4}$ pint) milk
1 small onion, sliced

1 small bay leaf
3 eggs, beaten
grated nutmeg
225 g (8 oz) asparagus tips
salt and pepper

Make the pastry, roll it out and line the baking tray with it.
Put the milk, onion, bay leaf, eggs, pinch of nutmeg in a
blender for a few seconds. Place the pastry-lined baking tray
on the grill. Put in the chicken pieces. Remove the tops
from the asparagus and place the sliced stems over the
chicken. Pour over this the blended ingredients.
Sprinkle the top with grated nutmeg. With the top
plate lowered, cook for 20 minutes. Check to see the
top of the flan does not stick to the grill. If it does,

leave the grill with the top open until the flan sets. Serve with asparagus tips as decoration in a star or flower shape on top of the flan.

Kathy's quick chicken special

Preheat automatic grills
Preheat temperature-controlled grills on highest number

4 chicken joints
225 g (8 oz) mushrooms, sliced
4 bacon rashers

100 g (4 oz) butter or margarine
tarragon
2 tablespoons white wine
salt and pepper

Lightly oil a baking tray. Also oil the chicken joints and put them in the tray on the grill. With the top plate lowered cook for 20 minutes. Open the grill, season the joints with salt and pepper. Cut slits in the centre of the joints and place a piece of butter or margarine into each slit. Add the mushrooms and bacon rashers to the tray and also sprinkle in the wine and tarragon. Cover the tray with baking foil which has been brushed lightly with oil. Lower the top of the grill and cook for a further 15 minutes until the chicken looks golden.

Left-over chicken supper

Preheat automatic grills
Preheat temperature-controlled grills on highest number

450 g (1 lb) minced
cooked chicken

1 packet (280 ml) cheese
sauce mix

50 g (2 oz) butter or
soft margarine

salt and pepper

450 g (1 lb) fresh or packet
mashed potatoes

breadcrumbs

1 egg, beaten

Form the minced cooked chicken into cutlet shapes. Dip them
in the beaten egg and coat with breadcrumbs. Oil a baking
tray and place the cutlets in it. Make up fresh cooked cheese
sauce or make according to the instructions on the packet.
Pour this over the cutlets. Season with salt and pepper. Cover
this with the cooked mashed potatoes. Dot the top of the
potato with butter or soft margarine. Cover the tray with
baking foil which has been brushed with oil. Place the tray
on the grill and, with the top lowered, cook for 5 minutes.
Open the grill. Remove the foil and, with the top plate again
lowered, cook for a further 4 minutes to brown the top.

Quick and easy chicken supreme

Preheat automatic grills
Preheat temperature-controlled grills Rima 901 No 4
Rima 903 No 2
Sunbeam No 4
Philips No 4

225 g (8 oz) tin asparagus tips
450 g (1 lb) tin chicken supreme
100 g (4 oz) cheddar cheese, grated
1 small onion, chopped

Place the asparagus and chopped onion in the baking tray.
Pour the tin of chicken supreme over the top and cover this
with the cheddar cheese. Place the tray on the grill and, with
the top plate lowered, cook for 4–5 minutes.

Chicken and vegetable casserole

Preheat automatic grills
Preheat temperature-controlled grills on highest number

2 cooking trays
½ chicken, cut into pieces
280 ml (½ pint) chicken
  stock or water
2 tablespoons white wine

1 small onion, sliced
1 carrot, sliced
1 bay leaf
salt and pepper

sauce
25 g (1 oz) butter or
  margarine
25 g (1 oz) plain flour

75 g (3 oz) mushrooms,
  sliced
salt and pepper
280 ml (½ pint) chicken
  stock

Place the cooking tray on the grill. Put in the chicken pieces
and add the stock and wine. Add the sliced onion, carrot and
bay leaf, salt and pepper. Cover the top with baking foil and,
with the top plate lowered, cook for 25 minutes until the
chicken is tender. Remove the chicken pieces and set aside.
Add the butter to the other baking tray and melt it. Stir in
the flour and cook with the top of the grill open until the
texture is smooth. Add the stock, mushrooms and, with the top
plate lowered, cook for a further 4–5 minutes. Season when
cooked. Pour this sauce over the chicken pieces and serve.

Chopped hardboiled egg or chopped ham are also delicious
in this sauce.

Duck drumsticks with orange and cinnamon

Preheat automatic grills
Preheat temperature-controlled grills on highest number

4 drumsticks (cut from a duck)
25 g (1 oz) flour
salt and pepper
2 tablespoons cooking oil

280 ml ($\frac{1}{2}$ pint) chicken stock from a cube
2 small oranges
powdered cinnamon
previously cooked rice

Wipe the drumsticks with a damp cloth. Mix together the flour, salt and pepper and coat the drumsticks with this. Place the baking tray on the grill. Pour in the oil, add the drumsticks and, with the top plate lowered, cook for 15–20 minutes, turning after the first 10 minutes. Open the grill and pour off the fat from the tray. Now add the chicken stock and the juice of one of the oranges. Close the grill and cook for 15 minutes. Serve the duck on a bed of cooked rice. Carefully remove the peel and pith from the other orange and slice the flesh thinly. Arrange these slices around the duck drumsticks and serve with the top lightly sprinkled with powdered cinnamon.

Meat

Grilled steak – three methods

Preheat automatic grills
Preheat temperature-controlled grills on highest number

steaks
salt and pepper for methods (b) and (c)
onions and/or mushrooms (optional)

(a) Brush the steaks with oil. Place them directly on the grill and, with the top plate lowered, cook for:
   3 minutes – rare
   5 minutes – medium
6–7 minutes – well done
Also take into account the thickness of the steaks. Season after cooking, this avoids bleeding the meat.

(b) Brush the steaks with oil, season with salt and pepper. Top with onions. Wrap in foil like a parcel. With the top plate lowered cook for 7–12 minutes, depending on meat thickness and personal taste.

(c) Prepare as method (b) but place the steaks in a well greased baking tray. With the top plate lowered, cook for 12–15 minutes, depending on thickness and personal taste. Mushrooms can also be added.

Steak with tomatoes and courgettes

Preheat automatic grills
Preheat temperature-controlled grills on highest number

1 large steak
100 g (4 oz) tomatoes,
 sliced

100 g (4 oz) courgettes,
 sliced
1 tablespoon butter
grated cheese

Lightly oil a baking tray. Put in the butter, tomatoes, courgettes and steak and place the tray on the grill. With the top plate lowered cook for 10 minutes. Cover the steak with cheese and cook for a further 2 minutes with the top plate lowered.

Pepper steaks

Preheat automatic grills
Preheat temperature-controlled grills on highest number

2 slices fillet or
 rump steak
3 teaspoons whole black
 peppercorns

50 g (2 oz) butter
1 tablespoon olive oil
1 teaspoon butter
2 teaspoons brandy

Trim and neaten the steaks, beat them with a meat tenderizer or use a rolling pin. Crush the peppercorns, again using a rolling pin or mortar and pestle. Press the crushed peppercorns into the steaks and leave aside for almost 1 hour. Place the butter and oil in the baking tray and, with the top plate lowered, heat butter quickly for about half a minute. Put in the steaks and cook with the top plate lowered for 6 minutes, turning once. Cook a little longer if steak is preferred well done. Remove from the tray and keep hot. Stir the brandy into the tray juices, lower the top of the grill to heat for 1 minute. Stir in the butter and pour the sauce over the steaks. Fresh green or red peppers can be used as a change from black peppercorns.

Carpetbagger steaks

Preheat automatic grills
Preheat temperature-controlled grills on highest number

4 thick pieces of fillet or rump steak	lemon juice
18 prepared mussels	salt and pepper
75 g (3 oz) butter	mushrooms, cooked
2 teaspoons chopped parsley	cooked tomatoes to garnish
	1 tablespoon parsley to garnish

Slit the steaks to make pockets, mix the mussels with half of the melted butter, the chopped parsley, a little lemon juice and seasoning. Put this into the steak pocket and skewer firmly or sew with double cotton thread. Brush the steaks with the remaining melted butter. Place them directly on the grill plates and cook with the top plate lowered, for about 5–7 minutes or until tender and suited to personal taste. Remove the skewers or thread, and serve garnished with cooked mushrooms, tomatoes and parsley. Oysters can be used in place of mussels.

Corned beef pastry

Preheat automatic grills
Preheat temperature-controlled grills on highest number

340 g (12 oz) corned beef	2 carrots, cooked and
1 medium onion, chopped	chopped
1 tablespoon oil	225 g (8 oz) shortcrust
salt and pepper	pastry
1 teaspoon tabasco sauce	50 g (2 oz) peas, cooked
1 egg, beaten	parsley

Flake the corned beef into a bowl. Cook the onion in the hot oil until soft and blend it with the corned beef. Add the seasoning, tabasco sauce, egg and vegetables. Roll out the pastry and line the baking tin with two-thirds of it. Cover with the filling and top with the rest of the pastry, keeping it under the top of the baking tin or dish. Decorate with leaves of the pastry made from the trimmings and glaze with beaten egg. With the top plate lowered, cook for 20 minutes. Serve hot or cold, garnished with parsley.

Beef rolls

Preheat automatic grills
Preheat temperature-controlled grills on highest number

680 kg (1½ lb) silverside	salt and pepper
of beef	1 carrot, peeled and sliced
mustard	25 g (1 oz) dripping
50 g (2 oz) fat ham	25 g (1 oz) plain flour
1 onion, finely chopped	280 ml (½ pint) water
6 cocktail sticks	

Tenderize the meat with a rolling pin or mallet, making it wafer thin. Cut into 6 slices. Spread the meat slices with mustard. Cut the fat ham into 6 long strips. Place some pieces of onion on top of the mustard with the beef, add the fat ham, salt and pepper, and roll up the meat, securing each individual portion lightly with cotton thread or cocktail sticks. Put the dripping in the baking tray, lower the top of the grill for $\frac{1}{2}$ minute then add the remaining onion and the carrot and cook for 5 minutes. Coat the meat with the flour and put it in the baking tray, adding the water at the same time. With the top plate lowered cook it for 40 minutes, stirring and adding a little water if necessary. Foil can be used to cover the tray for cooking. If you are using this method add 10 minutes to the cooking time.

Corned beef casserole

Preheat automatic grills
Preheat temperature-controlled grills on highest number

50 g (2 oz) lard
1 large onion, finely
 chopped
340 g (12 oz) tin corned
 beef

225 g (8 oz) potatoes,
 boiled and sliced
225 g (8 oz) tomatoes, peeled
150 ml ($\frac{1}{4}$ pint) beef stock
salt and pepper

Place the baking tray on the hot grill and add the lard and onion. Lower the top of the grill and cook for 3 minutes. Add the corned beef, potatoes and tomatoes, also pour over the stock and add seasoning. Lower the top of the grill and cook for 5 minutes. Open and cover the top of the baking tray with cooking foil. Again lower the top of the grill and cook for 20–25 minutes.

Old-fashioned beef casserole and dumplings

Preheat automatic grills
Preheat temperature-controlled grills on highest number

1 tablespoon butter or fat
225 g (8 oz) meat, cubed
1 tablespoon plain flour
1 medium onion, chopped
75 g (3 oz) turnip or
 courgettes, sliced

2 outside celery leaves,
 cut small
100 g (4 oz) carrot, cut
 chunky
1 teaspoon vinegar
280 ml (½ pint) stock

Roll the meat in the seasoned flour. Melt the fat or butter in a baking dish and add the meat cubes. Add the onion, turnip or courgettes, carrot, vinegar, stock and celery. Cover with buttered foil and cook for 30 minutes. Make the dumplings.

dumplings
100 g (4 oz) self-raising
 flour
1 teaspoon salt
50 g (2 oz) shredded suet

1 tablespoon parsley,
 chopped
4 tablespoons water

In a bowl mix all ingredients together lightly, keeping the mixture slightly dry. Roll into balls and place in the bubbling casserole. Cover again with the buttered foil. With the top plate lowered cook for a further 15 minutes.

Quickie beef and vegetable casserole

Preheat automatic grills
Preheat temperature-controlled grills on highest number

450 g (1 lb) rump steak
1 teaspoon cornflour
2 tablespoons oil
2 sticks celery, finely
 chopped

4 spring onions, finely
 chopped
100 g (4 oz) cabbage,
 finely shredded
1 tablespoon soya sauce
salt and pepper

Cut the meat into very thin slices. Mix the cornflour to a smooth paste with about 2 tablespoons of water. Add it to the beef and mix well until the beef is completely coated with the mixture. Put the oil in the baking tray and, with the top plate lowered, heat until the fat is hot (about 2 minutes), add the vegetables to the hot fat and again lower the top plate and cook for 5 minutes, stirring once. Add the meat, soya sauce, salt and pepper, mix well and add a little more oil if necessary. Don't let the meat get too dry. Cover the baking tray with cooking foil and cook for 6–7 minutes with the top plate lowered.

Burgundy beef casserole

Preheat automatic grills
Preheat temperature-controlled grills on highest number

340 g (12 oz) chuck steak	1 small onion, chopped
25 g (1 oz) bacon fat	50 g (2 oz) button
75 g (3 oz) unsmoked	mushrooms
streaky bacon, cut into	$\frac{1}{4}$ teaspoon mixed herbs
strips	150 ml ($\frac{1}{4}$ pint) stock
15 g ($\frac{1}{2}$ oz) flour	parsley
150 ml ($\frac{1}{4}$ pint) red wine	salt and pepper

Cut the steak into small cubes. Place the bacon strips and fat in the baking tray. Lower the top plate and cook for 2 minutes. Add the steak and again lower the top of the grill and cook for 4 minutes. Blend the flour in the fat in the baking tray. Lower the top plate and cook once more for 4 minutes. Stir in the stock and red wine. Again, lower the top plate and cook for another 4 minutes. Add the rest of the ingredients. Cover the baking tin with cooking foil and, with the top plate lowered, cook for 30–40 minutes or until tender.

Beef with prunes

Preheat automatic grills
Preheat temperature-controlled grills on highest number

280 ml (½ pint) brown
  stock
9 prunes or other fruits,
  sliced
340 g (12 oz) chuck steak
25 g (1 oz) flour

50 g (2 oz) cooking fat or
  dripping
1 tablespoon tomato purée
1 bay leaf
3 tomatoes, peeled
salt and pepper

Soak the prunes in the heated stock overnight. Tenderized
prunes can be used but soak for 1 hour only. Dice the meat
and coat it with the flour, season with salt and pepper. Put the
floured meat in the baking tray with the fat or dripping and,
with the top plate lowered, cook for 5 minutes. Add the
strained stock from the prunes to the meat. Again lower the
top of the cooker and cook for 6 minutes. Add the tomato
purée and the chopped prunes and bay leaf. Cover the tray
with cooking foil and cook for 15–20 minutes. Add the
tomatoes to the tray and season, again cover with foil and,
with the top plate lowered, cook for 10 minutes. Raisins,
apricots or peaches can be used in place of prunes.

Chilli con carne

Preheat automatic grills
Preheat temperature-controlled grills on highest number

450 g (1 lb) minced beef
100 g (4 oz) dried red
  kidney beans, soaked
  overnight
2 tablespoons corn oil
1 small green pepper,
  cored, seeded and
  chopped
1 onion, chopped

1 tablespoon mild chilli
  powder
½ teaspoon paprika
½ teaspoon ground cumin
1 tablespoon tomato purée
1 tablespoon flour
salt
400 g (14 oz) tin tomatoes

Cook the drained kidney beans in boiling salted water for
45 minutes until tender. Drain and preserve about half of the
water. Put the oil and chopped onion in the baking tray.
Lower the top of the grill and cook for 3–4 minutes. Add the
beef and chopped green pepper, lower the top of the grill
again and cook for 6 minutes, stirring twice to break up the
minced beef. Stir in the chilli powder, paprika, cumin,
tomato purée, flour and salt to taste. Lower the top plate and
cook for 3 minutes. Add the tomatoes and liquid straight from
the tin, also the beans, mixing thoroughly. Cover the baking
tray with cooking foil and, with the top plate lowered, cook
for 45 minutes until tender. Add the reserved bean water half
way through to prevent the meat drying and sticking. Add
more seasoning to required taste.

Topside slices in red wine

Preheat automatic grills
Preheat temperature-controlled grills on highest number

2 slices topside beef, cut
into 1 cm (½ in)
thicknesses
150 ml (¼ pint) red wine
1 small onion, chopped
1 small bay leaf
1 parsley sprig
thyme sprig, fresh or dried
½ teaspoon dried marjoram
25 g (1 oz) beef dripping
25 g (1 oz) flour
150 ml (¼ pint) beef stock
salt and pepper
100 g (4 oz) carrots, sliced
100 g (4 oz) spring onions
1 tablespoon parsley, chopped

Lay the beef slices in the baking tray. Add the chopped onion, herbs and wine. Leave aside to marinate in a cool place for 5–6 hours or overnight. Turn twice. Drain the meat, strain and reserve the marinade. Add the dripping to the meat and, with the top plate lowered, cook for 3 minutes. Add the flour and stir in the stock and reserved marinade. Leave the grill open and stir occasionally for 3–4 minutes. Cover with cooking foil and, with the top plate lowered, cook for 5 minutes. Add the carrots and spring onions. Sprinkle with salt and pepper. Re-cover with cooking foil. Again lower the top plate and cook for 45 minutes. Sprinkle some chopped parsley over the top when serving.

Pork chops – three methods

Preheat automatic grills
Preheat temperature-controlled grills on highest number

6 pork chops of equal thickness
salt and pepper if cooking directly between plates
stuffing mix for (b)
apple for (c)

(a) Place the seasoned pork chops directly on the grill, cook for 7–9 minutes.

(b) Alternatively, wrap the chops in foil with a choice of stuffing mix. Place directly between plates and cook for 15 minutes.

(c) Alternatively, place the chops in lightly oiled baking tray, add thinly sliced sweetened apple and, with the top plate lowered, cook for 20 minutes.

Pork chops – sweet'n'sour

Preheat automatic grills
Preheat temperature-controlled grills Rima 901 No 4
Rima 903 No 3
Philips No 4
Sunbeam No 4

4 pork chops
1 tablespoon cooking oil
450 g (1 lb) peach halves (tinned)
salt and pepper
100 g (4 oz) brown sugar
15 g ($\frac{1}{2}$ oz) plain flour
$\frac{1}{4}$ teaspoon mustard
$\frac{1}{4}$ teaspoon cinnamon
$\frac{1}{4}$ teaspoon powdered cloves
4 tablespoons white wine vinegar
280 ml ($\frac{1}{2}$ pint) water
50 g (2 oz) raisins
50 g (2 oz) crushed nuts
2 tablespoons soft margarine or butter
1 tablespoon sherry

Place the baking tray on the grill, pour in the oil and add the chops. With the top plate lowered cook the chops for 12 minutes. Now cook in a pan the water, sugar, mustard, cinnamon, cloves, vinegar and flour. Stir until the sauce thickens. Add the raisins and nuts, simmer for 15–20 minutes and add the butter and sherry. Place the chops on a warm serving plate with a peach half on top of each one and pour the sauce over them.

Sausage bake, country style

Preheat automatic grills
Preheat temperature-controlled grills on highest number

450 g (1 lb) pork or
 beef sausages
225 g (8 oz) carrots, sliced
1 large onion, sliced

1 tablespoon butter
salt and pepper
1 cup water

Place everything in a baking tray, arranging it to look
attractive. Cover with cooking foil and, with the top plate
lowered, cook for 20–25 minutes.

Grilled bacon and ale casserole

Preheat automatic grills
Preheat temperature-controlled grills on highest number

4 lean bacon chops
100 g (4 oz) brown sugar
½ teaspoon dry mustard
¼ teaspoon cinnamon
4 apricots or peach halves,
 or pineapple slices

100 g (4 oz) mushrooms,
 sliced
150 ml (¼ pint) dry cider,
 lager or beer

Lightly oil the baking tray. Put in the chops. Mix together
the sugar, mustard and spices, and sprinkle this over the
chops. Cover with the mushrooms. Add the fruit halves. Pour
over the cider or ale. Place the tray on the grill. Cover the
food with cooking foil and, with the top plate lowered, cook
for 20–30 minutes.

Sausage casserole

Preheat automatic grills
Preheat temperature-controlled grills on highest number

450 kg (1 lb) pork sausage
  meat
2 medium sized onions
1 medium sized green
  pepper, de-seeded

100 g (4 oz) celery
1 tablespoon butter
salt and pepper

Thinly slice the onion, celery and green pepper. Fry them in
the butter until tender. Spread half the sausage meat in the
baking tray and add the softened vegetables, salt and pepper,
and spread the remaining sausage meat on top. Lower the top
plate and cook for 30 minutes. Serve with mashed potatoes.

Grilled gammon steaks

Preheat automatic grills
Preheat temperature-controlled grills on highest number

2 gammon steaks
2 pineapple rings
2 eggs
salt and pepper
2 poaching rings

Trim the rind and some fat from the steaks. Put them on a
greased baking tin and into the grill and, with the top plate
lowered, cook for 5 minutes. Open the grill and turn over the
steaks. Close and cook for a further 3 minutes. Open the grill.
Place a pineapple ring on each steak then put one oiled
poaching ring on top of each pineapple ring. Break one egg
into each ring. With the top plate lowered, cook for 3–4
minutes. Scoop the eggs out of the poaching dishes and place
them on the top of the pineapple slices on each portion.

Gammon steaks

Preheat automatic grills
Preheat temperature-controlled grills Rima 901 No 3½
Rima 903 No 2
Philips No 3½
Sunbeam No 3½

4 gammon steaks
4 pineapple rings
50 g (2 oz) butter
2 tablespoons fresh
  parsley, chopped

4 teaspoons brown sugar
pinch of mustard
pepper
4 cherries

Snip off the fat around the steaks to prevent them curling.
Mix together the sugar, butter, mustard and parsley and
spread the mixture evenly over the gammon steaks. Place a
pineapple ring on top of each steak. Lightly brush the baking
tray with oil. Put the steaks in the tray and, with the top
plate lowered, cook for 10 minutes. Serve with a cherry in the
centre of the pineapple on each steak.

Braised chops

Preheat automatic grills
Preheat temperature-controlled grills on highest number

25 g (1 oz) oil
4 lamb or pork chops
1 medium onion, sliced
2 large sliced tomatoes
275 ml (½ pint) stock

salt and pepper
½ clove garlic
1 green pepper, de-seeded
  and chopped

Place the cooking tray on the grill. Add the oil, chops and
onion. With the top plate lowered cook for 5 minutes. Open
the grill. Add the stock, seasoning, garlic, tomatoes, and

green pepper. Again lower the top plate of the grill and cook for 30–40 minutes.

Lamb chops with ham

Preheat automatic grills
Preheat temperature-controlled grills on highest number

6 lamb chops	225 g (8 oz) large
1 tablespoon oil	mushrooms, peeled
salt and pepper	pinch garlic salt
6 slices ham	50 g (2 oz) butter
	juice of $\frac{1}{2}$ lemon

Trim the chops and place them on a baking tray. Pour in the oil. Cover the chops with the mushrooms, ham slices, salt, pepper and garlic salt. With the top plate lowered cook for 2 minutes. Add the butter and lemon juice. Cover with foil and, with the top plate lowered, cook for 15 minutes. Garnish with parsley and serve hot with peas and carrots.

Breast of lamb

Preheat automatic grills
Preheat temperature-controlled grills on highest number

225 g (8 oz) breast of lamb	100 g (4 oz) cleaned
1 small onion, sliced	mushrooms
2 tomatoes, skinned	salt and pepper
and sliced	

Cut the lamb into slices removing any bones. Put the slices in a lightly oiled baking tray and cover them with the onions, tomatoes, mushrooms, and season with salt and pepper. Place the tray on the grill and, with the top plate lowered, cook for 15 minutes.

Lamb chops in wine

Preheat automatic grills
Preheat temperature-controlled grills on highest number

6 lamb chops
225 g (8 oz) mushrooms
red wine
salt and pepper

Lightly oil the baking tray. Place the chops on it and cook
them for 5 minutes with the top plate lowered. Open the grill
and add the mushrooms and wine, enough to cover the base
of the baking tray. Season with salt and pepper. Cover with
cooking foil and cook for 15 minutes with the top plate
lowered.

Lamb and onion casserole

Preheat automatic grills
Preheat temperature-controlled grills on highest number

450 g (1 lb) lean lamb meat	50 g (2 oz) plain flour
2 tablespoons oil	1 tablespoon tomato purée
25 g (1 oz) butter	425 ml ($\frac{3}{4}$ pint) stock
2 onions, peeled and sliced	salt and pepper

Cut the meat into cubes of 2 cm (1 in). Place them in the
baking tray with the butter, oil and onions. Put the tray on
the grill and, with the top plate lowered, cook for 8 minutes,
opening the grill and turning once. Open the grill, stir in the
stock, flour, purée and seasoning. With the top plate lowered
cook for 30–40 minutes until tender.

Grilled lamb left-overs

Preheat automatic grills
Preheat temperature-controlled grills on highest number

450 g (1 lb) potatoes,
  cooked and mashed
pinch nutmeg
1 large onion, peeled and
  chopped
25 g (1 oz) dripping
25 g (1 oz) plain flour
280 ml (½ pint) stock

2 teaspoons tomato purée
225–285 g (8–10 oz)
  cold lamb, chopped
25–50 g (1–2 oz) cooked
  bacon, chopped
salt and pepper
25 g (1 oz) butter or
  margarine

Place the baking tray on the hot grill. Add the dripping and onion. With the top plate lowered cook for 4 minutes. Open the grill and add the flour. Close and cook until the onions are browning (2–3 minutes). Open the grill and stir in the stock and purée. Close and cook for a further 3 minutes. Open and add the lamb and bacon, lightly stirring it into the stock. Season to taste. Cover with mashed potatoes. Dot the top with a few small knobs of butter or margarine. With the top plate lowered cook for another 15 minutes.

Rolled escalopes of veal

Preheat automatic grills
Preheat temperature-controlled grills on highest number

6 veal escalopes
6 slices cooked ham
6 tablespoons cheddar cheese, grated

Beat the escalopes to tenderize them. Place a slice of ham on each escalope. Top the ham with the cheese. Roll up each escalope tightly and secure with cotton or cocktail sticks.

Place them on the oiled baking tray. With the top plate lowered cook for 10–12 minutes. Escalopes can be covered with buttered foil if desired before cooking.

Veal chops with mushrooms

Preheat automatic grills
Preheat temperature-controlled grills on highest number

4 veal chops	1 tablespoon brandy or
salt and pepper	red wine
1 teaspoon flour	1 tablespoon white wine
4 tablespoons oil	3 tablespoons double
40 g (1½ oz) butter or	cream
margarine	3 tablespoons parsley,
225 g (8 oz) mushrooms	chopped

Dust the chops with flour and season with salt and pepper. Put oil in the baking tray placed on the lower plate of the grill and when the oil is warm add the chops. Add the sliced mushrooms and wine. Cover with foil and, with the top plate lowered, cook for 20 minutes. Remove the chops to a warm serving dish. Add the cream to the mushrooms, and mix together. Pour the brandy on to the chops and light it. Pour on the cream and mushrooms to serve, and sprinkle with chopped parsley.

Escalopes Wiener schnitzel – two methods

Preheat automatic grills
Preheat temperature-controlled grills on highest number

4 escalopes beaten thinly	1 tablespoon butter
1 beaten egg	lemon wedges to garnish
breadcrumbs	

(a) Dip each escalope in beaten egg and coat with breadcrumbs. Melt the butter in the baking tray and add the escalopes. With the top plate lowered, cook for 5–7 minutes. Open the grill and turn the escalopes. Cook them for a further 5 minutes. Serve with lemon wedges.

(b) Brush the escalopes with oil or butter, season them with salt and pepper and wrap them in foil. Place them on the grill and, with the top plate lowered, cook for 5–7 minutes.

Kidneys in wine

Preheat automatic grills
Preheat temperature-controlled grills on highest number

8 lamb kidneys, skinned and chopped	salt and pepper
1 tablespoon butter	100 g (4 oz) mushrooms, sliced
1 medium sized onion, peeled and chopped	150 ml ($\frac{1}{4}$ pint) soured cream
1 tablespoon plain flour	boiled rice
5 tablespoons red wine	parsley
3 teaspoons Worcester sauce	

Melt the butter in the baking tray and cook the onion for 4–5 minutes with top plate lowered. Stir in the flour, add the kidneys, red wine, Worcester sauce, salt, pepper and mushrooms. With the top plate lowered cook for 3 minutes. Open and cover with buttered foil. Lower the top and cook for 7–10 minutes. Open again and add a little of the baking tray liquid to the soured cream (cream with a few drops of lemon juice added). Stir this back into the meat mixture and leave on the lower infra-red plate for 2 minutes. Serve on a bed of boiled rice. Sprinkle with some chopped parsley.

Devilled sheep's kidneys

Preheat automatic grills
Preheat temperature-controlled grills on highest number

4 sheep's kidneys
50 g (2 oz) butter or
  margarine

½ teaspoon French mustard
1 teaspoon Worcester sauce
pinch salt

Skin the kidneys. Split them in half and remove the cores.
Spread some of the soft butter or margarine over them and
salt to taste. Add a dot of mustard to each kidney. Put the
remainder of the butter in the baking tray and add the
Worcester sauce and prepared kidneys. Cover with foil and,
with the top plate lowered, cook for 4 minutes. Open the
grill, remove the foil and turn the kidneys. With the top plate
lowered cook for a further 3–4 minutes. Serve hot.

Braised liver or kidneys

Preheat automatic grills
Preheat temperature-controlled grills Rima 901 No 3½
                                        Rima 903 No 2
                                        Sunbeam No 3½
                                        Philips No 3½

450 g (1 lb) liver or
  kidneys, chopped and
  floured
50 g (2 oz) oil
1 medium sized onion

small tin tomato purée
280 ml (½ pint) stock
50 g (2 oz) sliced celery
  stalks
salt and pepper

Place the cooking tray on the grill. Add the oil, onion, liver or kidneys. With the top plate lowered, cook for 4–5 minutes. Open the grill and add the celery, tomato purée, stock, salt and pepper. Lower the top of the grill and cook for 30–40 minutes or until tender.

Rabbit casserole

Preheat automatic grills
Preheat temperature-controlled grills on highest number

4 rabbit joints	340 g (12 oz) potatoes,
seasoned flour	peeled and sliced
4 tablespoons (125 ml) oil	280 ml (½ pint) chicken stock
2 medium sized onions,	1 tablespoon parsley
peeled and sliced	salt and pepper

Roll the rabbit joints in the seasoned flour. Heat the oil in the baking tray and add the onions. Lower the top of the grill and cook for 3–4 minutes. Add the rabbit joints, turning them to brown evenly with the top plate lowered. Add the potatoes. Mix the stock and parsley and pour it over the rabbit joints. Season with salt and pepper. Cover with buttered foil, lower the top of the grill and cook for 25–30 minutes. Remove the foil, close the grill and cook for 3–5 minutes to brown slightly.

Mixed grill

Preheat automatic grills
Preheat temperature-controlled grills on highest number

oil	bacon
chipolata sausages	eggs
liver	tomatoes, sliced

Oil the baking tray and cook the chipolata sausages, with
the top plate lowered, for 4 minutes. Add the liver, lower the
top plate and cook for a further 3 minutes. Add the bacon
and eggs, lower the top plate and cook for a further 2
minutes. Add the tomatoes, lower the top plate and cook for
2 minutes.
Season after cooking.

Savoury snacks

Grilled bacon and tomato toasts

Preheat automatic grills
Preheat temperature-controlled grills on highest number

Lightly toast 2 slices of bread in the closed grill (takes about
1½ minutes). Spread the toast with butter. Place the toast in a
baking tray. Put some sliced tomato on the toast and cover
this with cheese. Decorate with chopped bacon. Put the tray
on the grill and, with the top plate lowered, cook for 3–4
minutes until golden brown and crisp.

Savoury bacon roll

Preheat automatic grills
Preheat temperature-controlled grills on highest number

225 g (8 oz) streaky bacon,
  chopped and cooked
1 small onion, chopped
1 teaspoon fresh parsley,
  chopped

½ teaspoon salt
100 g (4 oz) suet pastry
225 g (8 oz) flour
150 ml (¼ pint) cold water

suet pastry
Mix the flour, salt and chopped beef suet (or packet suet)
and add the water gradually to make a stiff dough. Turn the

56

dough on to a floured board. Knead very lightly and gently roll out an oblong shape. Lightly oil a baking tray and line it with pastry.

Mix the bacon, onion, parsley and salt together. Spread this over the pastry lining to within 1 cm ($\frac{1}{2}$ in) of the sides. Damp the edges with water and roll the whole thing up tightly. Place the tray on the grill and, with the top plate lowered, cook for 20–30 minutes. Serve with a hot, rich brown gravy.

Toasted sandwiches

Preheat automatic grills
Preheat temperature-controlled grills on highest number

Use thinly sliced white or brown bread
Butter one side of each slice
Place one slice *buttered side down* on the lower plate
Put the filling on top
Place the top slice on the filling with the *butter side up*
Close the grill and toast for 3–4 minutes.

fillings
(a) Spread the bread with mild mustard pickle. Add pre-cooked bacon and cheese.
(b) Spread with chutney. Add cheese and boiled ham.
(c) Place a slice of cheese on the toast and add raw onion rings.
(d) Place a slice of cheese on the toast and add some sliced tomatoes and sliced or chopped mushrooms.
(e) Spread with any kind of meat, pâté and fish paste.
There are any amount of fillings you can invent. These are just a few to give you some ideas.

Poached eggs

Preheat automatic grills
Preheat temperature-controlled grills on highest number

4 eggs
salt and pepper
paprika
parsley

4 poaching rings

Lightly grease a baking tray and place 4 lightly greased
poaching rings on it. Drop 1 egg in each ring. Pour a little
water in the baking tray, just enough to cover the base.
Lower the top plate of the grill and cook for 4 minutes until
the eggs are soft and white on top. Remove them from the
poaching rings. Serve, on warm toast, salt and pepper to
taste and garnish with parsley.

Scotch egg cakes

Preheat automatic grills
Preheat temperature-controlled grills on highest number

225 g (8 oz) sausage meat
a little oil
4 hardboiled eggs, sliced

4 tablespoons mayonnaise
capers
lemon segments

Shape the sausage meat into cake shapes and flatten them.
Lightly oil both sides and place them in the hot grill for
2 minutes. Top each cake with slices of hardboiled egg,
overlapping the slices. Top with mayonnaise. Garnish with
capers and serve with lemon segments.

French omelette

Preheat automatic grills
Preheat temperature-controlled grills on highest number

6 eggs
¾ teaspoon salt
dash pepper
40 g (1½ oz) butter

Lightly beat the eggs, just enough to mix the whites and
yolks. Add salt and pepper. Heat the butter in the baking tray
leaving the grill open. Pour a bit of the warm butter into the
beaten eggs, and reheat the remainder. Pour the eggs into the
baking tray. Replace the tray on the grill. Lower the top
plate and cook for 4–5 minutes. Serve immediately on heated
plates.

Puffy omelette

Preheat automatic grills
Preheat temperature-controlled grills on highest number

6 eggs, separated   dash pepper
6 tablespoons hot water   25 g (1 oz) butter
¾ teaspoon salt

Beat the egg whites until stiff and beat the yolks until they
thicken slightly. Add the hot water, salt and pepper. Fold the
yolks and whites together. Melt the butter in the baking tray
on the open grill. Tip the pan so that the sides are greased.
Turn the egg mixture into the baking tray. Lower the top
plate of the grill and cook until the omelette is light and
fluffy, about 4–5 minutes. Slip a spatula under the omelette
to loosen it and flip it out on to a warm serving plate
immediately.

Bacon and tomato flan

Preheat automatic grills
Preheat temperature-controlled grills on highest number

225 g (8 oz) shortcrust
 pastry
2 eggs
2 tablespoons milk
salt and pepper

4 rashers bacon, chopped
2 medium-sized tomatoes,
 sliced
parsley

Line the baking tray with the uncooked shortcrust pastry. Cut
the bacon into small pieces. Beat the eggs, milk, salt, pepper
and bacon. Pour the mixture into the flan and put the
tomatoes on top to decorate. Place the baking tray on the
grill and, with the top plate lowered, cook for 15–20 minutes
until the filling has set. Garnish with sprigs of parsley.

Cheese and onion flan

Preheat automatic grills
Preheat temperature-controlled grills on highest number

225 g (8 oz) onions,
 peeled and chopped
20 g ($\frac{3}{4}$ oz) butter
$\frac{1}{2}$ tablespoon oil
2 eggs

2 baking trays

3 tablespoons double cream
100 g (4 oz) cheese, grated
salt and pepper
225 g (8 oz) shortcrust
 pastry

Sauté the onions in oil and butter in a baking tray under a
closed grill, for 3 minutes. Line the other baking tray with
the uncooked shortcrust pastry. Whip the eggs, cream,
grated cheese, salt and pepper together. Add the cooked
onions and pour the mixture into the pastry lined tray. Put
on the grill and, with top plate lowered, cook for 15–20
minutes or until the filling has set.

Cheddar bake

Preheat automatic grills
Preheat temperature-controlled grills on highest number

4 large potatoes, baked
100 g (4 oz) cheddar
  cheese, thinly sliced

salt and pepper
chopped parsley

Slice the potatoes in two, lengthways. Prick them all over with a fork, and season them. Lay slices of cheese over the potatoes. Place in a tray on the grill and, with the top plate lowered, cook for 3–4 minutes. Serve decorated with the parsley.

Spud bake

Preheat automatic grills
Preheat temperature-controlled grills on highest number

4 medium sized potatoes,
  cooked and sliced
75 g (3 oz) soft margarine
100 g (4 oz) cheddar
  cheese, grated

2 tablespoons parmesan
  cheese, grated
salt and pepper

Put the potatoes into a baking tray, arranging the slices in rows. Mix together the margarine, cheddar cheese, parmesan cheese, salt and pepper. Spread fairly thickly over the potatoes. Place on the grill and, with the top plate lowered, cook for 5–7 minutes.

Ratatouille

Preheat automatic grills
Preheat temperature-controlled grills on highest number

2 medium sized aubergines
2 tablespoons oil
2 medium onions, sliced
1 green pepper, seeded
 and sliced
1 red pepper, seeded and
 sliced

3 courgettes, sliced
4 ripe tomatoes, skinned
 and sliced
salt and pepper
chopped parsley

Slice the aubergines and arrange them in a baking tray. Cover
with salt and set aside for 30 minutes. Cover with the oil. Add
the onions and sweet peppers. Cover with cooking foil and,
with the top plate lowered for about 10 minutes, cook until
the vegetables are soft. Add the courgettes, tomatoes and
seasoning, and put back the foil. Again, lower the top plate
and cook for a further 10 minutes. Turn the food into a
warm serving dish and garnish with parsley. Ratatouille can
be served cold as a starter, or eaten with meat.

Desserts

Baked apples

Preheat automatic grills
Preheat temperature-controlled grills Rima 901 No 4
                                      Rima 903 No 3
                                      Sunbeam No 5
                                      Philips No 5

4 large apples, cored and
  halved horizontally
100 g (4 oz) sultanas
4 tablespoons water

100 g (4 oz) castor sugar
hot custard or
  fresh cream and
  chopped nuts

Place the apple halves on a baking tray and fill the centre
holes with sultanas. Pour the water into the bottom of a
baking tray and add the sugar. Place the tray on the grill
and cook with the top plate lowered, for 8–10 minutes until
the apples are cooked but not too soft. Serve with hot
custard or cover with a little fresh cream and chopped nuts.

Blackberry and apple crumble
(other fruit can be used in recipe)

Preheat automatic grills
Preheat temperature-controlled grills on highest number

63

225 g (8 oz) cooking apples
1 teaspoon allspice
100 g (4 oz) granulated
  sugar
100 g (4 oz) blackberries

175 g (6 oz) plain flour
pinch salt
75 g (3 oz) butter or
  margarine
4 tablespoons brown sugar

Peel, core and slice the apples. Place on a lightly greased baking tray. Sprinkle with the allspice and some of the granulated sugar. Cover the apples with the blackberries and the remaining granulated sugar. Sieve the flour into a bowl, and add the salt. Rub the butter or margarine into the flour until the mixture looks like breadcrumbs. Sprinkle the mixture over the fruit and then sprinkle the brown sugar over the top. Cover the tray with some lightly greased cooking foil. With the top plate lowered cook in the grill for 15–20 minutes. Serve with whipped cream or custard.

Apple charlotte

Preheat automatic grills
Preheat temperature-controlled grills on highest number

175 g (6 oz) breadcrumbs
50 g (2 oz) beef suet,
  shredded
grated rind of 1 lemon

340 g (12 oz) cooking apples,
  sliced
75 g (3 oz) sugar

Grease the baking tray well. Mix the breadcrumbs, suet, and lemon rind. Line the baking tray with a little of this mixture and fill the dish with alternate layers of the sliced apple and sugar, and breadcrumb mixture, finished up with the breadcrumbs. Cover the tray with buttered foil and cook, with top plate lowered, for 20–25 minutes.

Apple fruit crumble

Preheat automatic grills
Preheat temperature-controlled grills Rima 901 No 4
                                                                           Rima 903 No 3
                                                                           Philips No 4
                                                                           Sunbeam No 4

680 g (1½ lb) apples, sliced	100 g (4 oz) sugar
100 g (4 oz) soft margarine	1 teaspoon cinnamon
175 g (6 oz) flour	50 g (2 oz) preserved ginger, chopped

Sieve the flour into a bowl and rub in the margarine until the mixture resembles breadcrumbs. Stir in the sugar, cinnamon and ginger. Sprinkle this mixture on top of the prepared fruit in the baking tray. Place the baking tray on the grill and, with the top plate lowered, bake for 15–20 minutes. Keep checking to make sure the crumble top is not browning too much. Serve hot or cold with custard or cream, or both.

Apple pie

Preheat automatic grills
Preheat temperature-controlled grills on highest number

340 g (12 oz) shortcrust pastry	apple pie spice or cinnamon
3 large cooking apples, peeled, cored and sliced	1 egg, beaten
2 tablespoons brown sugar	icing sugar
	2 tablespoons water

Roll out two-thirds of the pastry and line a greased baking tray with it. Place the apples in the baking tray. Sprinkle with brown sugar and apple pie spice or cinnamon. Add the water. Roll out the remaining pastry and use to cover the pie and seal the edges 1 cm ($\frac{1}{2}$ in) from the top of the baking tray. Glaze the top with the beaten egg. Cover with buttered cooking foil and, with the top plate lowered, cook for 20–25 minutes.

Serve hot or cold, dusted with icing or confectioners sugar.

Hot scotch bananas

Preheat automatic grills
Preheat temperature-controlled grills on highest number

4 bananas, sliced thickly
100 g (4 oz) brown sugar
2 tablespoons lemon juice

2 tablespoons scotch whisky
cream

Put the bananas in the baking tray. Sprinkle with the sugar, lemon juice and whisky. With the top plate lowered cook for 5 minutes.

Serve hot with cream.

Jamaican bananas

Preheat automatic grills
Preheat temperature-controlled grills on highest number

1 banana, sliced thickly
1 teaspoon/5 ml orange
 juice
1 teaspoon/5 ml lemon juice

1 teaspoon brown sugar
1 pinch cinnamon
1 teaspoon/5 ml rum

Mix the banana into the orange and lemon juice until well coated. Pour the banana on to the centre of a large piece of foil, add the sugar, cinnamon and rum. Fold up the foil to make a parcel. Fold the edges together to seal and place the parcel in a baking tray. With the top plate lowered cook for 5 minutes until hot and the sugar has melted. Serve 1 parcel to each person. Brandy can be used in place of rum.

Bread and butter pudding

Preheat automatic grills
Preheat temperature-controlled grills on highest number

4 slices bread, buttered
 on one side
75 g (3 oz) raisins
1 tablespoon castor sugar

ground nutmeg
280 ml (½ pint) milk
2 eggs

Remove any crusts on the bread and cut the slices into quarters. Put half the bread into the well greased baking tray. Sprinkle with the fruit and sugar. Cover with the remaining bread, butter side upwards. Beat the eggs and milk together and strain it through a piece of muslin or a fine sieve on to the bread and butter. Sprinkle the top with nutmeg and leave standing for 30 minutes. Place the baking tray on the grill and lower the top plate. Cook for 15 minutes or until firm.

Crumbly bread pudding

Preheat automatic grills
Preheat temperature-controlled grills on highest number

340 g (12 oz) bread scraps
100 g (4 oz) demerara sugar
100 g (4 oz) currants and
 sultanas
2 teaspoons grated orange
 rind

2 teaspoons mixed spice
50 g (2 oz) shredded suet
2 eggs, beaten
castor sugar
custard

Tear the bread into small pieces and put it in a bowl. Cover with boiling water. Soak for 20 minutes then drain and squeeze the bread to crumble it. Mash it well with a fork. Stir in the other ingredients, keeping back the castor sugar and custard. Grease the baking tray and spread the mixture in it. Place the tray on the grill and, with the top plate lowered, cook for 20 minutes or until the top is brown and crisp. Serve, covered with castor sugar and hot custard.

Cheese or curd pie

Preheat automatic grills
Preheat temperature-controlled grills on highest number

100 g (4 oz) shortcrust
pastry
225 g (8 oz) cottage
cheese or curds
280 ml (½ pint) milk, hand
hot, with 1 teaspoon
rennet essence added

50 g (2 oz) castor sugar
50 g (2 oz) currants
1 egg
40 g (1½ oz) soft margarine
pinch cinnamon
pinch ground nutmeg

Line an 18 cm (7 in)-square sandwich tin, with thin pastry. Melt the margarine and mix in all the other ingredients. Fill the flan with the mixture. Place the tin on the grill and, with the top plate lowered, cook for 10 minutes.

Quick cinnamon custard tart

Preheat automatic grills
Preheat temperature-controlled grills on highest number

225 g (8 oz) shortcrust
 pastry
280 ml (½ pint) milk

2 eggs
25 g (1 oz) castor sugar
powdered cinnamon

Line a baking tray with the pastry. Warm the milk in a pan –
do not let it boil. Lightly beat the eggs and sugar together.
Add the milk and pour into the pastry case. Sprinkle
cinnamon on the top. Place the tray on the grill and, with
the top plate lowered, cook for 15–20 minutes until set – if
browning too quickly leave the top of the grill open and let it
set gently for 5–7 minutes.

Quick coconut tart

Preheat automatic grills
Preheat temperature-controlled grills on highest number

225 g (8 oz) shortcrust
 pastry
3 tablespoons jam
½ cup coconut

2 cups cooked custard
1 tablespoon sugar
grated nutmeg

Line a baking tray with the uncooked pastry. Spread the
inside with the jam. Pour the custard over the jam. Sprinkle
generously with coconut. Cover with a sprinkling of ground
nutmeg which has been mixed with the sugar. Place the tray
on the grill and, with the top plate lowered, cook for 5–7
minutes until lightly browned.
Serve cold or hot, with double cream.

Quick crunchie pudding

Preheat automatic grills
Preheat temperature-controlled grills Rima 901 No 4
                                            Rima 900 No 3
                                            Philips No 4
                                            Sunbeam No 4

25 g (1 oz) butter	2 cups cooked custard
25 g (1 oz) cornflakes	1 cooking apple, grated
25 g (1 oz) demerara sugar	or finely chopped

Lightly grease an 18 cm (7 in) baking tray. Pour the custard into the tray. Spread the fruit over it. In a saucepan melt the butter and stir in the sugar and cornflakes. Pour this mixture over the fruit in the baking tray. Place the tray on the grill and, with the top plate lowered, cook for 7–10 minutes. Serve hot, with cream if desired.

Custard pie

Preheat automatic grills
Preheat temperature-controlled grills Rima 901 No 4
                                            Rima 903 No 3
                                            Philips No 4
                                            Sunbeam No 4

100 g (4 oz) shortcrust	280 ml (½ pint) milk
pastry	2 tablespoons castor sugar
2 eggs	grated nutmeg

Line an 18 cm (7 in) baking tray with thin pastry. In a bowl whisk the eggs. Bring the milk and sugar to boil in a pan, and then pour on to the eggs and stir. Pour the mixture into the pastry case. Grate some nutmeg over the top of the custard. Place the baking tin on the grill and, with the top plate lowered, cook for 15 minutes or until set.

Fruit crunchie

Preheat automatic grills
Preheat temperature-controlled grills on highest number

50 g (2 oz) melted butter
  or margarine
50 g (2 oz) digestive
  biscuits, crushed

50 g (2 oz) sugar
450 g (1 lb) rhubarb,
  fresh or tinned
½ level teaspoon cinnamon

Mix together the butter, biscuits and half of the sugar. If using fresh rhubarb wipe it and cut it into small pieces. Place these in a baking tray, sprinkle with cinnamon and the remaining sugar. Cover with buttered cooking foil and, with the top plate lowered, cook for 10 minutes. Cover the top with the biscuit mixture and serve hot or cold, with fresh cream.

Jam or fruit turnovers

Preheat automatic grills
Preheat temperature-controlled grills on highest number

100 g (4 oz) puff pastry
4 tablespoons jam or soft fruit, cooked
1 egg, beaten
castor or icing sugar

Roll out the pastry to form a 25 cm (10 in) square and divide it into four squares. Place 1 tablespoon of the jam or soft cooked fruit in the centre of each square. Fold one corner over to the other to form the squares into triangles, sealing the edges with some of the beaten egg. Glaze the tops lightly with the remaining beaten egg. Place in a well greased baking tray on the lower plate of the grill and, with the top plate lowered, cook for about 8 minutes. Serve hot sprinkled with castor or icing sugar.

Grilled mincemeat tart

Preheat automatic grills
Preheat temperature-controlled grills on highest number

340 g (12 oz) puff pastry
225 g (8 oz) mincemeat
1 egg, beaten

Roll out most of the pastry to fit into a baking tray. Spread on the mincemeat to 1 cm ($\frac{1}{2}$ in) from the edge all the way round, pinch the edges to neaten. Roll out the remaining pastry into strips. Place the strips over the mincemeat in lattice style. Glaze with the egg. Put the tray on the grill and, with the top plate lowered, cook for 8–10 minutes.

Pastry

Rich shortcrust pastry

225 g (8 oz) plain flour
125 g (4 oz) butter or lard
½ teaspoon baking powder

½ teaspoon salt
1 beaten egg
water

Sieve the flour, baking powder and salt into a bowl. Rub the butter into the flour until the mixture resembles fine breadcrumbs. Mix in the egg. Add a little water if the mixture is too dry. Turn the pastry on to a floured board. Knead lightly, then roll out to the size required. This is pastry which melts in the mouth.

Shortcrust pastry

225 g (8 oz) plain flour
½ teaspoon salt
125 g (4 oz) fat
2 tablespoons water

Sieve the flour and salt into a bowl. Cut the fat into small pieces and rub it into the flour until the mixture resembles fine breadcrumbs. Add the water, mixing with a round-bladed knife until the mixture binds together. Gather the pastry up into a ball and it should leave the bowl clean. Turn it out on to a floured board. Roll out until the dough is smooth.

Fork mix pastry

150 g (5 oz) soft margarine
225 g (8 oz) plain flour
2 tablespoons water

Sieve half the flour into a mixing bowl. Add the margarine
and water. Mix with a fork, blending the ingredients together.
Stir in the remaining flour to form a dough. Turn this on to a
lightly floured board and knead until the dough is smooth.
Roll out and use as desired.

Yorkshire pudding

Preheat automatic grills
Preheat temperature-controlled grills on highest number

125 g (4 oz) plain flour
pinch salt
1 egg
280 ml (½ pint) milk

Sieve the flour and salt into a mixing bowl. Make a well in
the centre and drop in the egg. Add a little of the milk and
beat until a smooth batter is obtained. Gradually add the
rest of the milk. Melt a small piece of butter in a baking tray
on the lower plate of the grill. Pour in the batter and, with
the top plate lowered, cook for 10–12 minutes.

Flan pastry

Preheat automatic grills
Preheat temperature-controlled grills on high setting

100 g (4 oz) plain flour
50 g (2 oz) butter or margarine
50 g (2 oz) castor sugar
1 large egg yolk

Sieve the flour straight on to the working surface. Make a
well in the centre and add the butter or margarine, sugar and
egg yolk. Work everything together with your fingertips then
work in all the flour to form a dough. Lightly knead the
dough into a ball and place in a polythene bag. Put it into
the refrigerator for ½ hour. Roll out and use as desired.
This pastry is most suitable as sweet pastry and can be
cooked blind on a grill in the following way:
Line a baking tin with the pastry. Press some cooking foil
well down on to the pastry. Place the tin on the lower plate
of the grill. Lower the top plate and cook for 6–7 minutes.
This is how to cook all blind pastry on a grill.

Hot water pastry or raised pie crust

225 g (8 oz) plain flour
50 g (2 oz) lard
115 ml (4 fl oz) hot water or milk
½ teaspoon salt

Sieve the flour and salt into a basin. Put the water and lard
into a pan and when boiling pour the liquid over the dry
ingredients. Mix together with a spoon, and when cool
enough turn on to a floured board and knead until smooth.
Form quickly into the shape required.

Rough puff pastry

225 g (8 oz) plain flour
½ teaspoon salt
100 g (4 oz) butter

few drops lemon juice
cold water

Sieve the flour and salt into a bowl. Add the lemon juice and the butter, broken into pieces the size of a walnut. Add sufficient cold water to make the mixture stick together. Turn the pastry out on to a floured board and roll it into a long strip. Fold it in three, and press the edges together. Half turn the pastry, and again roll it into a strip, fold in three and repeat this until the pastry has had four rolls, folds and half turns. It is then ready for use. Rough puff pastry is suitable for meat pies, patties, sausage rolls, etc.

Note: if a richer pastry is desired use 170 g (6 oz) butter to 225 g (8 oz) flour. Half butter and half lard may be used.

Cakes, scones and biscuits

Victoria sandwich

Preheat automatic grills
Preheat temperature-controlled grills on highest number

100 g (4 oz) soft margarine
100 g (4 oz) soft brown
 sugar
150 g (6 oz) self-raising
 flour

1 teaspoon baking powder
2 large eggs, beaten
jam

In a bowl cream together the margarine and sugar. Sift the flour and baking powder and gradually add it with the eggs to creamed mixture. Beat the mixture until it is well blended. Grease and line the baking tray with greaseproof paper. With the top plate lowered, cook for 8–10 minutes until firm to touch.

for fruit and cherry cake
Add 50 g (2 oz) sultanas
   50 g (2 oz) glacé cherries

Cook for 10–12 minutes.

Fatless sponge cake

Preheat automatic grills
Preheat temperature-controlled grills on highest number

2 eggs
50 g (2 oz) castor sugar
100 g (4 oz) self-raising
 flour

icing sugar
chocolate or coconut, grated

Line the base of a baking tray with greaseproof paper. Whisk
the eggs and sugar together. If desired use a blender and
whisk until the mixture is thickening. Lightly fold in the flour.
Pour the mixture into the prepared baking tray. With the
top plate lowered cook for 5–7 minutes until the sponge is
firm to touch. Turn out to cool on wire rack. Dust top with
icing sugar or mix 1 cup of icing sugar with very little water
to make a stiff icing. Spread this over the top of the cake.
Sprinkle with grated chocolate or coconut.

Grilled and baked jam sponge

Preheat automatic grills
Preheat temperature-controlled grills on highest number

225 g (8 oz) jam
100 g (4 oz) castor sugar
100 g (4 oz) self-raising
 flour
1 teaspoon baking powder

$\frac{1}{4}$ teaspoon salt
75 g (3 oz) soft margarine
2 eggs
2 tablespoons cold water

Grease the baking tray. Spread the jam over it. Put all the
remaining ingredients into a bowl and mix them together
well with a wooden spoon. Spread this mixture over the jam,

making the top smooth. Place the tray on the grill and, with the top plate lowered, cook for 8–10 minutes. Serve with hot custard.

Quick ginger cake

Preheat automatic grills
Preheat temperature-controlled grills on highest number

225 g (8 oz) plain flour
1 teaspoon baking powder
¼ teaspoon salt
150 g (5 oz) soft margarine
200 g (7 oz) castor sugar

3 eggs
4 tablespoons milk
3 teaspoons ground ginger
25 g (1 oz) sliced ginger
few walnuts

Sieve together the flour, baking powder, and salt. Add the margarine, sugar, eggs, milk and ground ginger and beat with a wooden spoon for 1–2 minutes until it is of a smooth, soft consistency. Grease and flour the baking tray. Pour in the mixture. Place sliced ginger pieces, and if desired, a few walnuts on top. With the top plate lowered cook for 15–20 minutes.

Simple and easy chocolate cake

Preheat automatic grills
Preheat temperature-controlled grills on highest number

175 g (6 oz) castor sugar
175 g (6 oz) soft margarine
3 beaten eggs
150 g (5 oz) self-raising
  flour

25 g (1 oz) cocoa powder
1 tablespoon syrup
2 tablespoons milk

Cream together the margarine and sugar. Add the eggs, syrup, sifted flour, cocoa powder and milk. Mix together and spread into two 18 cm (7 in)-square cake trays, which have already been lightly greased and floured. Cook with top plate lowered. After 5 minutes, open and check. If not quite cooked give extra time.

Picnic fruit cake

Preheat automatic grills
Preheat temperature-controlled grills Rima 901 No 4
                                       Rima 903 No 3
                                       Philips No 4
                                       Sunbeam No 5

225 g (8 oz) self-raising   4 tablespoons milk
 flour   150 g (5 oz) dried fruit
150 g (5 oz) sugar   (eg raisins and sultanas)
2 eggs

Put all the ingredients, except the fruit, in a bowl and mix for 1–2 minutes until smooth and creamy. Add the fruit. Lightly grease the baking tray and spread the mixture in it. Place the tray on the grill, lower the top plate and cook for 15–20 minutes on small automatic grills. Allow an extra 5–10 minutes on temperature-controlled grills.

Christening or anniversary cake

Preheat automatic grills
Preheat temperature-controlled grills on highest number

175 g (6 oz) butter
175 g (6 oz) dark-brown
  sugar
3 large eggs, beaten
½ level teaspoon mixed
  spice
pinch salt
1 level tablespoon dark
  treacle

225 g (8 oz) plain flour
25 g (1 oz) chopped
  walnuts
50 g (2 oz) glacé cherries,
  halved
100 g (4 oz) sultanas
100 g (4 oz) raisins
175 g (6 oz) currants
2 tablespoons rum or brandy

1 baking tray size 25cm × 20cm × 5cm (10in × 8in × 2in)

Brush the cake tin with some melted fat or butter. Line the tray with 2 sheets of greaseproof paper, fitting to the exact size of the tray. Wrap some cooking foil round the outside of the tray.

Mix together all the dried fruits, cherries and chopped nuts. Soak the mixture in rum or brandy overnight, covering the bowl with a clean cloth.

Sift together the flour, salt and spice. Cream the butter, sugar and treacle. Beat in the eggs. Gradually add the soaked fruit to this treacle mixture, beating lightly as you go. Finally fold in the flour, salt and spices. Press into the lined tray smoothing the top flat. Cover with some lightly buttered greaseproof paper (doubled) and cover again, placing a piece of baking foil over the greaseproof paper. Put the baking tray on the grill and, with the top plate lowered, cook for 1–1¼ hours until a skewer pressed into the cake comes out clean. Cake can be covered with marzipan and decorated with icing.

Cherry cake

Preheat automatic grills
Preheat temperature-controlled grills on highest number

100 g (4 oz) soft margarine
100 g (4 oz) castor sugar
150 g (6 oz) self-raising
 flour
3 large eggs
pinch salt

75 g (3 oz) glacé cherries,
 halved
rind of ½ lemon, grated
4 tablespoons icing sugar
lemon juice
coconut, grated

Cream the margarine and sugar together, gradually add the
beaten egg. Sift the flour and salt. Fold in the sifted flour.
Add the grated rind of lemon and also the cherries. Lightly
grease and flour a baking tray and spread the mixture in it.
Place the tray on the grill and, with the top plate lowered,
cook for 12–15 minutes. To ice, sift the icing sugar into a
bowl and mix it to a thin paste with a little lemon juice. Add
colouring if desired. Spread over the cake and sprinkle with
coconut and dot with half a glacé cherry.

Heavenly cake

Preheat automatic grills
Preheat temperature-controlled grills on highest number

50 g (2 oz) soft brown
 sugar
75 g (3 oz) soft margarine
2 egg yolks

150 g (6 oz) self-raising
 flour
1 teaspoon vanilla essence

topping
2 egg whites
100 g (4 oz) castor sugar
25 g (1 oz) glacé cherries,
 chopped

25 g (1 oz) coconut
25 g (1 oz) walnuts, chopped
1 teaspoon vanilla essence

Cream the margarine and sugar together. Beat in each egg
yolk separately. Fold in the flour and vanilla essence. Lightly
grease and flour the baking tray. Spread the mixture in the
tray leaving the top smooth. Place the tray on the grill and,

with the top plate lowered, cook for 7–10 minutes, or until firm to touch.

topping
Whisk the egg whites stiffly and fold in the sugar. Then stir in the rest of the ingredients. Spread the mixture on top of the cake and return to the grill. With the top plate lowered cook for a further 5–7 minutes until the top is golden. Cut the cake into fingers when cool.

Quick economy cheese cake

Preheat automatic grills
Preheat temperature-controlled grills on highest number

225 g (8 oz) rich
  shortcrust pastry
2 eggs and their weight in
  butter, sugar and flour

½ teaspoon baking powder
a little jam
grated lemon rind

Line a greased baking tray with the rolled out pastry. Spread the jam evenly over the bottom. Cream the butter and sugar in a bowl and add the beaten egg with a little of the flour. Add the remainder of the flour with the baking powder and lemon rind. Mix well and spread over the top of the jam. Place the tray on the grill and, with the top plate lowered, cook for 15–20 minutes until the top browns. If the cake is not set when the top is brown leave the top plate of the grill open until it is set, leaving the tray sitting on the bottom plate.

Date and rhubarb cake

Preheat automatic grills
Preheat temperature-controlled grills on highest number

200 g (8 oz) self-raising
  flour
125 g (5 oz) sugar
100 g (4 oz) soft margarine
100 g (4 oz) chopped dates

200 g (8 oz) rhubarb,
  chopped small
2 eggs
milk
icing sugar

In a bowl cream the margarine and sugar, mix in the
remainder of ingredients, except the icing sugar, adding
some milk last to make a soft consistency. Grease or oil the
baking tray and spread the mixture in it. Place on the grill
and with the top plate lowered, cook for 12–15 minutes until
the top is lightly browning. Spread the top with icing sugar.

Raisin rhapsody

Preheat automatic grills
Preheat temperature-controlled grills on highest number

225 g (8 oz) shortcrust
  pastry
225 g (8 oz) raisins
2 tablespoons self-raising
  flour

1 egg
50 g (2 oz) soft margarine
$\frac{1}{2}$ cup castor sugar
icing sugar

Melt the margarine in a pan. Add the sugar, raisins and flour.
Stir in the beaten egg and mix everything thoroughly together.
Slightly grease or oil the baking tray and line it with the
thinly rolled out pastry. Spread the mixture over this, place
the tray on the grill and, with the top plate lowered, cook for
15–20 minutes. When cool cover with sifted icing sugar and
cut into fingers.

Rock buns

Preheat automatic grills
Preheat temperature-controlled grills on highest number

225 g (8 oz) self-raising
  flour
100 g (4 oz) castor sugar
100 g (4 oz) margarine

75 g (3 oz) coconut
1 egg, beaten
a little milk

Mix the flour and sugar in a bowl. Rub in the margarine
until the mixture resembles breadcrumbs. Mix in the coconut,
egg and a little milk to make a fairly stiff dough. Lightly oil
a baking tray. Put the mixture on to the baking tray in small
heaps. Place on the grill and, with the top plate lowered,
cook for 10–12 minutes or until the buns are lightly browned.

Kathy's economy treacle scones

Preheat automatic grills
Preheat temperature-controlled grills on highest number

225 g (8 oz) self-raising flour
½ teaspoon salt
1 tablespoon treacle
milk or buttermilk

Sieve together the flour and salt. Mix in the treacle until the
mixture resembles breadcrumbs. Stir in the milk to make a
soft, elastic dough. Toss out on to a floured board. Flour the
top of the dough. Press the dough out lightly by hand and
cut it into 4 large scones. Place the scones on a floured baking
tray. Lower the top of the grill and cook for 10 minutes.
When cool spread with butter.

Cheese scones

Preheat automatic grills
Preheat temperature-controlled grills on highest number

175 g (6 oz) self-raising
  flour
40 g (1½ oz) soft margarine
75 g (3 oz) grated cheese

1 beaten egg
2 tablespoons milk
pinch salt and pepper
pinch powdered mustard

In a bowl rub the margarine into the flour. Add the grated
cheese, pepper, salt and powdered mustard. Mix in the egg
and milk. Roll out the dough on a floured board to 1.5 cm
(½ in) thick. Cut it into triangles. Brush the tops lightly with
grated cheese. Put them on a lightly floured baking tray and
place on the grill. With the top plate lowered cook for 10
minutes.

Almond fingers

Preheat automatic grills
Preheat temperature-controlled grills Rima 901 No 4½
                                       Rima 903 No 3
                                       Philips No 4½
                                       Sunbeam No 4½

200 g (8 oz) shortcrust
  pastry
100 g (4 oz) icing sugar
50 g (2 oz) castor sugar

¼ teaspoon cinnamon
1 cup chopped nuts
2 egg whites

Lightly grease or brush the baking tray with oil and line it
with the rolled out shortcrust pastry. Mix everything else
together in a bowl. Spread the mixture on the pastry. Place
the tray on the grill and, with the top plate lowered, cook for
15 minutes. Cut it into fingers when cold.

Quick economy biscuit tin filler

Preheat automatic grills
Preheat temperature-controlled grills on highest number

170 g (6 oz) soft margarine
1 tablespoon golden syrup
100 g (4 oz) demerara sugar
225 g (8 oz) porridge oats

Grease a baking tray. Melt the margarine, syrup and sugar
in a pan. Stir in the rolled oats. Spread the mixture evenly
into the baking tray. Place the tray on the grill and, with the
top plate lowered, cook for 10–12 minutes until golden brown.
Cut into fingers or squares while warm. Remove from the
tray when cold.

Wheatmeal biscuits

Preheat automatic grills
Preheat temperature-controlled grills on highest number

225 g (8 oz) wheatmeal
  flour
25 g (1 oz) castor sugar
150 g (5 oz) butter

1 beaten egg
$\frac{1}{2}$ teaspoon vanilla essence
chocolate (optional)

Mix flour and sugar together in a bowl, rub in the butter
until it resembles breadcrumbs. Add the egg and essence and
mix to a stiff paste. Roll out on floured board 1 cm ($\frac{1}{2}$ in)
thick. Cut into rounds. Place on a lightly greased baking
tray. (This takes half the quantity of biscuits at one time.)
Place the tray on the grill and, with the top plate lowered,
cook for 10–15 minutes. When cold, spread one side with
melted chocolate if desired.

American biscuits

Preheat automatic grills
Preheat temperature-controlled grills on highest number

100 g (4 oz) butter
450 g (1 lb) plain flour
140 ml ($\frac{1}{4}$ pint) milk
140 ml ($\frac{1}{4}$ pint) water

In a bowl rub the butter into the flour and mix well with the milk and water. Knead the dough well. Lightly oil a baking tray and press the dough in it. With the top plate lowered cook for 20 minutes, lightly browning the top. Cut into fingers and cool in tray. These biscuits can be eaten with savouries.

Quick and simple almond fingers

Preheat automatic grills
Preheat temperature-controlled grills on highest number

170 g (6 oz) self-raising flour
170 g (6 oz) semolina or ground rice
170 g (6 oz) castor sugar

170 g (6 oz) soft margarine
1 small egg and 1 large egg
1 teaspoon almond essence
jam
25 g (1 oz) flaked almonds

In a bowl mix together everything except the jam and flaked almonds to a stiff paste. Turn the dough on to a lightly floured board and knead it. Divide the mixture into two. Press half the mixture into a greased baking tray. Spread this with a little jam. Spread the rest of the mixture on top of the jam, then sprinkle on the flaked almonds. Place the tray on the grill and, with the top plate lowered, cook for 12 minutes, until turning golden brown. Leave to cool and cut into fingers.

Melting moments

Preheat automatic grills
Preheat temperature-controlled grills on highest number

100 g (4 oz) butter
75 g (3 oz) brown sugar
200 g (7 oz) rolled oats
1 handful of lightly crushed cornflakes

Cream the butter and sugar together. Add the oats and mix
well. Lightly grease a baking tray and press the mixture well
down into it, smoothing the top. Press the cornflakes in
evenly all over. With the top plate lowered, cook for 10–12
minutes. Cut into fingers or squares while the mixture is still
warm. Leave these to get quite cold before removing them
from the tray.

Quick malt slice

Preheat automatic grills
Preheat temperature-controlled grills on highest number

225 g (8 oz) digestive biscuits, crushed
225 g (8 oz) melted margarine
225 g (8 oz) condensed milk
1 tablespoon golden syrup

Melt the margarine. Add the biscuits and other ingredients.
Lightly grease a baking tray. Spread mixture in it and press
well down. Place on the grill and, with the top plate lowered,
cook for 5 minutes.

Crunchie treat for tea-time

Preheat automatic grills
Preheat temperature-controlled grills on highest number

100 g (4 oz) soft margarine
100 g (4 oz) castor sugar
1 tablespoon golden syrup

100 g (4 oz) cornflakes
50 g (2 oz) porridge oats

Heat the margarine, sugar and syrup in a saucepan and stir
in the cornflakes and oats. Press the mixture into a well
greased baking tray. Place the tray on the grill and, with the
top plate lowered, cook for 6–8 minutes until golden brown.
Leave to cool and cut into fingers.

Grilled ginger crunch biscuits

Preheat automatic grills
Preheat temperature-controlled grills on highest number

100 g (4 oz) soft margarine
1 dessertspoon golden
 syrup
75 g (3 oz) demerara
 sugar

100 g (4 oz) self-raising
 flour
100 g (4 oz) porridge oats
1 small teaspoon ground
 ginger
pinch of salt

2 baking trays

In a baking tray put the margarine and syrup and lower the
top plate of the grill over the tray for one minute. In a bowl
sift the flour, oats, sugar, salt and ginger. Open the grill and
pour the melted mixture into the dry ingredients in the bowl.
Mix them together thoroughly. Grease the other baking tray
and spread the mixture over this. Place it on the grill and,
with the top plate lowered, cook for 10 minutes. Cut into

fingers while warm and leave these in the tray until they are cool and crisp.

Scotch shortbread

Preheat automatic grills
Preheat temperature-controlled grills on highest number

170 g (6 oz) butter
75 g (3 oz) castor sugar
225 g (8 oz) plain flour

Cream together the butter and sugar. Add the flour and mix thoroughly using your warm hand to bind the mixture together and leave the bowl clean. Press the mixture into a baking tray. With the top plate lowered, cook for 10–15 minutes, until pale brown. Cut while warm, into fingers. Leave these to cool in the tray.

Australian crunchie triangles

Preheat automatic grills
Preheat temperature-controlled grills on highest number

Rima 901 No 4
Rima 903 No 3
Philips No 4
Sunbeam No 4

225 g (8 oz) soft margarine
150 g (5 oz) castor sugar
75 g (3 oz) coconut
1 tablespoon cocoa powder

60 g ($2\frac{1}{2}$ oz) crushed cornflakes
170 g (6 oz) self-raising flour

Melt the margarine in a pan, stir in the sugar, cocoa, coconut and cornflakes. Gradually stir in the flour. Lightly oil a baking tray and spread the mixture in it pressing it down and keeping the top level. Place tray in grill and, with the top plate lowered, cook for 10–12 minutes. Cut into triangles while still warm. When cold cover with melted chocolate, if desired.

Grilled syrup tarts

Preheat automatic grills
Preheat temperature-controlled grills on highest number

170 g (6 oz) shortcrust pastry

filling
3 tablespoons fresh breadcrumbs
3 tablespoons warmed golden syrup
juice of small lemon

Line a baking tray with the shortcrust pastry rolled out thin. Mix together the breadcrumbs, syrup and lemon juice. Spread the mixture over the pastry. Decorate the top, if desired, with any left-over pastry. Place the tray on the grill and, with the top plate lowered, cook for 10 minutes.

Viennese fingers

Preheat automatic grills
Preheat temperature-controlled grills on highest number

40 g (1½ oz) icing sugar, sieved
100 g (4 oz) soft margarine
100 g (4 oz) plain flour
50 g (2 oz) plain chocolate, melted

butter icing
75 g (3 oz) soft margarine
225 g (8 oz) icing sugar, sieved
2–3 tablespoons milk

Cream together the icing sugar and margarine. Stir in the flour. Spoon the mixture into a piping bag fitted with a star nozzle. Pipe the mixture on to the baking tray in fingers. Place the tray on the grill and, with the top plate lowered, cook for about 7 minutes. Cool on a wire tray. This quantity should make 2 tray loads. Sandwich the fingers together, in pairs, with the butter icing in the centre. Dip each end of the Viennese Fingers in the melted chocolate and leave to set.

Griddle

A griddle is a cooking utensil known as *girdle* in Scotland where it has been used for centuries.

This method of baking and cooking is spreading throughout the world as people increasingly cook and eat a variety of foreign food.

The Hartington infra-red grill has a griddle. Simply remove the grill plates by releasing the front clip. This now exposes the flat griddle plate. Very lightly oil it before use. Follow the instructions carefully and the results will be delicious.

Bacon and egg

Remove grill plates and preheat griddle

4 rashers bacon
2 eggs
2 tomatoes, halved

Place the rashers of bacon on the dry griddle plate. Lower the top plate and cook for 1 minute. Drop the eggs on the griddle plate with the pre-cooked bacon pushed to the sides. Cook the eggs for 1–2 minutes, until they are set. Tomatoes, if desired, can be cooked with the eggs, turning them once.

Cheese dreams

Remove grill plates and preheat griddle

4 slices bread
butter or margarine
50 g (2 oz) cheddar cheese, thinly sliced

Spread 4 slices of bread with butter or margarine. Place 2 slices on the griddle plate with the butter sides *down*. Place the slices of cheese on top of these and then the other 2 bread slices with their butter sides *up*. Lower the top plate of the griddle and toast for half a minute.

This can be cooked with ham, tomatoes, pâté or any filling of your choice.

Drop pancakes

Remove grill plates and preheat griddle

100 g (4 oz) self-raising flour
1½ tablespoons castor sugar
1 teaspoon baking powder
2 eggs
milk

Sift the flour, sugar and baking powder in a bowl. Make a well in the centre and break the eggs into it, stirring until all the flour is drawn in from the sides. Add the milk and beat the mixture to a smooth dropping consistency, free from lumps. Drop the batter a tablespoonful at a time on to the hot griddle and cook until bubbles begin to form. Turn over each of the pancakes before the bubbles burst and cook for another minute or so until both sides are brown.

Serve hot or cold with butter and jam. If eating them cold allow to cool, wrapped in a clean teacloth. This keeps them soft.

Plain griddle scones

Remove grill plates and preheat griddle

225 g (8 oz) self-raising flour
50 g (2 oz) soft margarine

1 tablespoon castor sugar
¼ teaspoon salt
150 ml (¼ pint) milk

In a bowl sift the flour and salt together. Rub in the margarine. Add the sugar and gradually mix in sufficient milk to make an elastic dough. Gather the dough together with your fingertips and turn it onto a floured board. Knead it lightly and roll out. Cut rounds of about 2 cm (¾ in) thick and cook each side for about 5 minutes on the griddle until brown.

Girdle scones

Remove grill plates and preheat griddle

225 g (8 oz) self-raising flour
¼ teaspoon salt
50 g (2 oz) lard

50 g (2 oz) castor sugar
1 beaten egg
150 ml (¼ pint) milk

In a bowl mix together the flour and salt. Rub the lard in to make a breadcrumb texture. Mix in the sugar. Add the milk and egg quickly with a wooden spoon, until all the flour is absorbed. Turn the dough out on a well floured board. Divide it into three pieces, do not *knead*. Handle the dough as little as possible. Roll out into 6 mm (¼ in) thickness and divide each round into four.

Bake on a well greased griddle for 4 minutes on each side.

Fruit muffins

Remove grill plates and preheat griddle

225 g (8 oz) self-raising flour
1 teaspoon baking powder
pinch salt

50 g (2 oz) lard
75 g (3 oz) butter
100 g (4 oz) currants
milk

In a bowl sift the flour, salt and baking powder together and rub in the lard and butter. Add the currants and sufficient milk to make an elastic dough. Roll this out and cut it into rounds of about 6 mm (¼ in) thick. Cook each side for 4–5 minutes on the hot griddle plate. Split each muffin in half and serve hot with butter.

Treacle scones

Remove grill plates and preheat griddle

175 g (6 oz) self-raising flour
½ teaspoon baking powder
pinch salt

75 g (3 oz) treacle
50 g (2 oz) soft margarine
150 ml (¼ pint) milk

Sift the flour, baking powder and salt in a bowl. Rub in the margarine. Drop in the treacle and mix until the mixture resembles breadcrumbs. Add the milk to form a soft dough and roll this out on a floured board. Cut into triangular shapes about 2 cm (¾ in) thick and cook each side for about 5 minutes on the hot griddle.

Wholemeal scones

Remove grill plates and preheat griddle

175 g (6 oz) wholemeal
flour
50 g (2 oz) plain flour
50 g (2 oz) margarine

2 teaspoons baking powder
¼ teaspoon salt
200 ml (⅓ pint) milk

Sieve the flour, salt and baking powder into a bowl three
times. Rub in the margarine until the mixture resembles
breadcrumbs. Mix well and add the milk. Turn the dough on
to a floured board. Knead it just enough to bind it and then roll
it out. Cut it into rounds about 2 cm (¾ in) thick and cook
each side for about 5 minutes on the hot griddle.

Fruit scones

Remove grill plates and preheat griddle

100 g (4 oz) plain flour
½ teaspoon bicarbonate of
soda
1 teaspoon cream of tartar
50 g (2 oz) seedless raisins

1 egg, beaten
1 tablespoon castor sugar
25 g (1 oz) butter
150 ml (¼ pint) milk

In a bowl sift the flour, cream of tartar and soda. Rub the
butter into this. Mix in the fruit and sugar. Add the egg and
the milk and form the mixture into a soft dough. Roll this out
on a floured board and cut it into rounds about 2 cm (¾ in)
thick. Cook each side for about 5 minutes on the hot griddle
until brown.

Parkins

Remove grill plates and preheat griddle

50 g (2 oz) soft margarine
100 g (4 oz) fine oatmeal
2 tablespoons castor sugar
1 egg, beaten
2 tablespoons treacle

100 g (4 oz) plain flour
1 level teaspoon powdered
  ginger
milk

In a bowl mix together the oatmeal, ginger and flour. Stir in
the melted margarine, sugar and treacle. Add the beaten egg
and sufficient milk to make a thick, dropping consistency.
Drop the mixture, a tablespoon at a time, on to the hot
griddle and cook each side for about 2 minutes until firm
and brown.
Cool on a wire tray.

Welsh griddle cakes

Remove grill plates and preheat griddle

225 g (8 oz) self-raising
  flour
1 teaspoon baking powder
½ teaspoon salt
100 g (4 oz) soft margarine

50 g (2 oz) castor sugar
50 g (2 oz) currants
1 egg, beaten
2 tablespoons milk

In a basin mix the flour, baking powder and salt. Rub in the
margarine until the mixture resembles breadcrumbs. Add the
sugar and currants. Mix to a fairly stiff dough with the egg
and milk. Roll the dough out thinly on a floured board. Cut
into rounds with a 5 cm (2 in) cutter. Bake on a hot, well
greased griddle for 3–4 minutes on each side.

Potato cakes

Remove grill plates and preheat griddle

170 g (6 oz) boiled
  potatoes, sieved
100 g (4 oz) plain flour
75 g (3 oz) margarine

2 teaspoons baking powder
¼ teaspoon salt
milk

In a bowl sift the flour, baking powder and salt. Rub in the margarine and mix in the sieved potatoes as lightly as possible. Add sufficient milk to bind everything together. Roll the mixture out on a floured board and cut it into rounds or triangles 6 cm (3 in) thick. Cook each side for 4–5 minutes on the griddle until the cakes are brown.

Potato scones

Remove grill plates and preheat griddle

170 g (6 oz) boiled
  potatoes, sieved
100 g (4 oz) plain flour
75 g (3 oz) soft margarine

2 teaspoons baking powder
¼ teaspoon salt
a little milk

Sift the flour, baking powder and salt together. Rub in the margarine and mix in the sieved potatoes as lightly as possible. Add sufficient milk to bind everything together. Roll out the dough on to a floured board and cut it into rounds or squares, cutting from corner to corner to form triangles 6 cm (3 in) thick. Place on a dry griddle plate and, with the top plate lowered, cook for 4–5 minutes until the scones are browning.

Bannocks

Remove grill plates and preheat griddle

170 g (6 oz) medium
  oatmeal
170 g (6 oz) plain flour

150 ml ($\frac{1}{4}$ pint) milk
$\frac{1}{2}$ teaspoon salt
1 level teaspoon cream of
  tartar

Mix the dry ingredients together thoroughly and stir in the
milk to make a soft dough. Divide the mixture into 4 pieces
and roll out each piece into a 1 cm ($\frac{1}{2}$ in) thickness. Put this
on the griddle and lower the top plate, cooking for about
4 minutes, to make sure the bannock is cooked right through.

Index

103

Rita G. Springer
Caribbean Cookbook £1.50

Rita Springer, a leading expert on every aspect of Caribbean food,
presents a whole spectrum of mouthwatering recipes, reflecting the
influence of European, American and Chinese food as well as the
traditional recipes of the islands. Includes a chapter on Caribbean kitchen
equipment, a helpful glossary, and details of how to obtain the more
unusual ingredients from British suppliers.

'Exciting cooking' SUN

Anne and Jane Cope
Leatherwork £2.95

The natural good looks and wearing qualities of leather make it one of
the most appealing of craft materials. With an increasing number of
suppliers of skins and tools, leatherwork is no longer a difficult craft to
take up.

This clear, step-by-step guide explains the technical language of
leatherwork, the different kinds and uses of leather, with sections on how
to dye and tool leather and make a whole range of clothing, bags, belts
and even simple soft furnishings.

Ann Stearns
Crochet £2.95

A craft book to explain both the techniques of crochet and the more
complex stitches for textured designs, illustrated with photographs
for step-by-step guidance and colour illustrations of finished crochet
work. There are suggestions of simple designs to start on before making
your own designs, and information on the wide range of textures and yarns
available.

Arthur Eperon
Traveller's France £1.75

Six major routes across France, taking in the best restaurants and hotels, visiting the most interesting out-of-the-way places. This detailed and up-to-the-minute handbook is for the traveller who wants more out of France than a mad dash down the motorway. Each of the six routes across the country is illustrated with a specially commissioned two-colour map, and includes a host of information on where to eat and drink, where to take children, where to stay, and how to get the most out of the towns and countryside.

C. E. Lucas Phillips
The New Small Garden £2.50

For many years *The Small Garden* has been acclaimed as the one essential book for every gardener. Now C. E. Lucas Phillips' bestselling handbook has been completely revised and adapted. Illustrated in colour and black and white, *The New Small Gardener* will become the classic guide to getting the best out of the average garden today.

David Lewis
The Secret Language of Your Child £1.50

Children can communicate before they have learned to speak. This fascinating book tells how they use this 'secret language' and what it means.

'A language of looks and gestures that can be even more eloquent than the most fluent speech' TIMES EDUCATIONAL SUPPLEMENT

'A book with a serious and important purpose ... an excellent book and, what is more, fun' PSYCHOLOGY TODAY

Cook Books

☐	**The Infra-Red Cook Book**	Kathy Barnes	£1.25p
☐	**All About Cookery**	Mrs Beeton	£1.50p
☐	**The Microwave Cook Book**	Carol Bowen	£1.25p
☐	**Pressure Cooking**	Kathleen Broughton	£1.50p
☐	**The New Casserole Treasury**	Lousene Rousseau Brunner	£1.00p
☐	**Gail Duff's Vegetarian Cookbook**	Gail Duff	£2.25p
☐	**Cooking on a Shoestring**		£1.95p
☐	**A Taste of Ireland**		£2.25p
☐	**A Taste of London**		£1.95p
☐	**A Taste of Paris**		£1.75p
☐	**A Taste of Scotland**	Theodora FitzGibbon	£1.95p
☐	**A Taste of Wales**		£1.50p
☐	**A Taste of Yorkshire**		£1.95p
☐	**Cuisine Minceur**	Michel Guérard	£1.50p
☐	**Cordon Bleu Book of Jams, Preserves and Pickles**	Rosemary Hume and Muriel Downes	90p
☐	**The Best Bread Book**	Patricia Jacobs	70p
☐	**Quick and Easy Chinese Cooking**	Kenneth Lo	£1.50p
☐	**Learning to Cook**	Marguerite Patten	95p
☐	**Traditional French Cooking**	Jennie Reekie	60p
☐	**The Potato Cookbook**	Gwen Robyns	£1.50p
☐	**Complete International Jewish Cookbook**	Evelyn Rose	£1.50p
☐	**The Constance Spry Cookery Book**	Constance Spry	£5.95p
☐	**The Times Cookery Book**	Katie Stewart	£1.75p
☐	**Eat Well and Be Slim**	Marika Hanbury Tenison	80p
☐	**Mediterranean Cooking**	Paula Wolfert	£1.95p

All these books are available at your local bookshop or newsagent, or can be ordered direct from the publisher. Indicate the number of copies required and fill in the form below

Name_____
(block letters please)
Address_____

Send to Pan Books (CS Department), Cavaye Place, London SW10 9PG
Please enclose remittance to the value of the cover price plus :

25p for the first book plus 10p per copy for each additional book ordered to a maximum charge of £1.05 to cover postage and packing
Applicable only in the UK

While every effort is made to keep prices low, it is sometimes necessary to increase prices at short notice. Pan Books reserve the right to show on covers and charge new retail prices which may differ from those advertised in the text or elsewhere